In the Company of Writers 2008

Meadow Brook Writing Project 2008 Summer Institute

iUniverse, Inc.
NEW YORK   BLOOMINGTON

In the Company of Writers 2008

Original drawings by Matthew Brown

iUniverse books may be ordered through booksellers or by contacting:

iUniverse
1663 Liberty Drive
Bloomington, IN 47403
www.iuniverse.com
1-800-Authors (1-800-288-4677)

Because of the dynamic nature of the Internet, any Web addresses or links contained in this book
may have changed since publication and may no longer be valid.

ISBN: 978-1-4401-9398-9 (sc)
ISBN: 978-1-4401-9399-6 (ebk)

Printed in the United States of America

iUniverse rev. date: 12/8/2009

CONTENTS

ACKNOWLEDGEMENTS

We would like to express our appreciation to our directors, John Callahan, Mary Cox, Marshall Kitchens and Kathleen Reddy-Butkovich, for creating an atmosphere that fostered creativity without judgment. Thank you for your enthusiasm, support and encouragement.

We would like to thank Cori Rice and Cliff and Kathleen Lawson for their assistance with the graphics, formatting, and other tasks that also helped to make this book possible.

For several weeks this summer, the contributors to this book wrote volumes as they delved into the various aspects of life that most of us, at times, encounter. While the robotic routine is familiar to all, these writers saw the whimsical, surreal, humorous, serious, and spiritual in spite of the audacious advancement of time. Through deep introspection, the writers of this book took a serious bite out of life, and we invite our readers to do the same.

Laura Gabrion
Cornelia Pokrzywa
Rebecca Rivard

FOREWORD

It was the summer of heart and bee attacks,
Women crushing men in pools,
e-Baying by the light of the moon,
Ouija boards and canoe trips,
Spider-Man and soldiers,
Marathons and lessons well learned,
Shoeless grandfathers,
Anthropomorphic purses,
And The Badlands by Dawn Fawn Vaughn.
We were led by a Renaissance woman,
A Vygotskian scholar,
A woman of Wondrous Words,
And an affable cyber-techie who twitters.
It was the summer of the Meadow Brook Writing Project 2008,
In which we were strung together like friendship bracelets,
One that will linger.

Rebecca Rivard

CHAPTER 1

POETRY

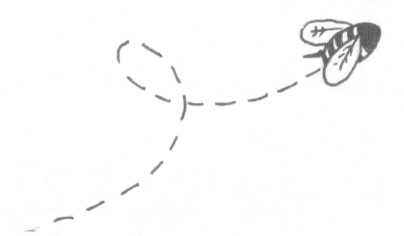

SATURDAYS

Alexandra Adamus

I like Saturdays—
the best.
You can drink coffee
from Starbuck's
and add sugar
and cream
and more sugar
and lots of chocolate.
And know you have
the entire day
to lounge
and read
and shop
and work on
never ending projects
or do whatever.
And go to Eastern Market
with your sister-in-law
and buy plants
and be happy
all the time
not only in the mornings with coffee,
but the entire Saturday.

I Am From

Alexandra Adamus

I am from all places: Europe, Ontario, out west, and the mid-west.
I am from the inner city and the outer country--
From grime and cleanliness, from grassless yards to over-grown mountain sides.

I am from engineers and architects, intellectuals and farmers with thirteen children.
I am from all fathers and grandfathers named Robert--
And all women small and strong.

I am from sewing and craft projects, quilts and finger puppets.
I am from coming in with the most creative Halloween costume--
And then having family members guess who I am.

I am from the unusual and the peculiar, the understanding and the tolerant.
I am from animal loving, tree hugging, the radical...the sensible and the sometimes not
so sensible...from both tradition and exploration.

I am from found objects, movie critics, and ice cream socials.
I am from big long meals and endless dinner conversation.
I am from a crazy loving family of true acceptance.

ACT TWO: WILL WE MISS THEM?

Alexandra Adamus

When I sit peacefully and reflectively in the garden near the gate—
and drink my tea and eat my cake
I watch the birds, butterflies, and bees—
each doing its own business with such ease.
This year I can't help but notice—
that there are fewer bees buzzing among us.
What is up?
First the Monarch butterflies, and now the bees?

Could it be true, what some scientists say—
and this is very much to my dismay.
That bees are the canaries for the human race,
and are disappearing very quickly without a trace?

Some mention mites that carry a deadly virus—
that hurt the bee and leave it feeling near dead.
Whole colonies get sick and infected—
not leaving much in the hive to be connected.

Now something even more serious has come along—
and believe me this is much more than silly sing-song.
Whole bee colonies are disappearing at an alarming rate—
Only the queen and the babies are left to their own terrible fate.

Between you and me—
I think this awful thing is called CCD.
If this is the case—
there will no bees left to pollinate.

Beekeepers turned truck driver—
haul their bees across the country through pesticide fields--
to pollinate 90% of flowering crops we eat for our meals.
What's that you say?
You'll just eat steak everyday?

Well, cows eat alfalfa, a flowering plant too.

When they are all long gone—
be sure to ask the people in places like Hong Kong.
What it is they have to do—
to have their plants and trees grow food.

With all this talk of gloom and doom—
and how things may never again bloom.
Just remember when we die of starvation,
There will be no flowers to send to our funerals.

Global warming, cell signals, and lots of stress--
I'm sure like us, that bees are doing their very best.
I can't help but ask myself—
What have we done to our world?

Obviously, something bad enough
that prevents the bees from finding their way home.

WHERE I'M FROM

Patricia Bieber

I'm from the bungalow on Kensington Street sheltered and cooled by
giant maples and oaks,
I'm from piles of leaves, jumped in and scattered and piled up again.
I'm from Grandma Morneau's house on Laprairie and sleepovers and
good-night prayers said on our knees.
I'm from spoolies and perms, Easter bonnets and lacey dresses, worn
under spring coats holding small pink corsages.
I'm from summers spent in dusty old barns on tire swings in hay lofts
at Uncle Ray's farm.
I'm from warm summer days, spent sprawled 'cross my bed, reading
and dreaming of what lies ahead.
I'm from "go play", and "be home when the streetlights come on" and
a twig across the legs when I didn't.
I'm from deep faith and five "Our Father's," and five "Hail Mary's,""no
talking in church," and "kneel up straight."
I'm from school uniforms and knee socks and "Yes, Sister," and "No,
Sister."
I'm from Frances and Chuck and the smell of strong coffee and dad
making oatmeal on a cold winter's morning,
From "Patricia Ann!" and "keep it down" and
tomato soup with grilled cheese sandwiches.

I'm from stories and fond memories, love and strong shoulders, wisdom
and brave hearts.
I'm from all of these moments –
eternally blessed.

Two Friends in a Canoe

Patricia Bieber

Two friends, in a canoe
paddling their way
down the Au Sable.
Men load the canoe, thinking they're daft,
for bringing enough supplies
to survive a nuclear blast.
One sits forward one sits aft,
Pat's in the front and Phyllis's in the back.
Launched by a push from the men on the bank,
The canoe pounces forward like a cat on attack.
Heading down river at break-neck speed,
Pat's in the back with Phyllis in the lead.
Two friends, in a canoe,
paddling backwards
down the Au Sable.
Twisting and turning, this way and that,
Phyllis turns the canoe like a cat turns a rat.
Gently they paddle, round curves and round bends,
steering 'tween rocks and under huge limbs.
Rounding a bend, there's a limb hanging low,
home to a spider, an itsy, bitsy foe.
Phyll gaped at the spider, screamed and stood up,
ready to do battle; no giving up.
Raising her oar, she pounded the limb,
sending that small spider into oblivion.
Two friends, in a canoe,
rocking and pitching
on the Au Sable.
Out spills Pat, like water from a cup,
spluttering and spitting, trying to stand up.
Slipping and sliding on river-smoothed rocks,
She wades to the bank, with wet jeans and soaked socks.
Phyllis paddles over, with a canoe full of water,
John and Paul yell, "Hey, what's the matter?"

"We dumped the canoe!" The two women shout.
Husbands to the rescue, they dump the water out.
Two friends in a canoe
continue to paddle
down the Au Sable.
Memories were made, on the river that day,
two friends grow closer day by day.

HOLDING ON, LETTING GO

John Callaghan

People are asking me,
"When are you retiring?"
I have no answer, but some
Things I want to hold on to-

In his journal, Shawn rages
Against his ex-girlfriend:
"You two-timing spider
Splattered on a dirty windshield."

Nora is finishing a book on
Her own for the first time,
A Child Called "It,"

The tears on her cheeks
Bright wet beads of grief
And guilt. She writes, "I'll
Never pinch my little brat
Brother's nose again."

Patrick interviews Great
Grandpapa about Pearl Harbor,
About when the bombs came.
Patrick quotes Great Grandpapa
In his paper:
"Back then the only good Jap
Was a dead Jap. Now they
Make damn good cars."

Some things I'm letting
Go:

The administrator says,
"I don't believe in sit

And git" and talks for
An hour and a half.
Thank God for naps,
Little blessings that
Snore away the verbiage.

A colleague says to mc,
"You say your students write
All year long. How come
They still can't write a
Decent sentence?"
I want to say, "Because
You won't allow them."
But I don't. I'm letting
Go.

 I just want to hold on,
To nourish:

Andrew and Justin,
Sierra and Samantha,
My students
Who have grown like snow-crowned
Pine trees in a desert.

All the other stuff:
I'm letting go.

CHILD OF WAR

Linda DeCumen

Wandering the streets, reaching for help
      the lost child
We look away.

The cry at night and during the day,
the lost child
We look away.

The hope of love, praying for peace
      the lost child
We look away.

Memories linger, home up in smoke
      the lost child
We look away.

The plea for crumbs, debris everywhere
      the lost child
We look away.

The empty eyes, the expressionless stare
      the lost child
We look away.

The loss of a mother, a father, a brother
      the lost child
We look away.

The explosions sound, dead bodies everywhere
      the lost child
We look away.

The loneliness, deafening sound of quiet
      the lost child

We look away.

Barefoot, torn shirts, urine-stained pants
        the lost child
We look away.

Desperation filled streets, rats eating flesh
        the lost child
We look away.

Hoping for love, praying for peace
        the lost child
We look away.

The future is dying, God takes a small hand
        the lost child
We look away.

Death becomes triumph, tears dry and fade
        the lost child
We look away.

Will you give, will you help
        the lost child
Don't look away.

DRIVERS BEWARE

Linda DeCumen

Oh look though yonder car doth lie,
It's Marshall Kitchens texting by.

He ran through neon flickering lights
While facebooking, he lost conscious sight.

The philosophy, "Everyone drive with care,"
went out the window when twittering with a stare.

The sign looked blurry and indiscreet
As Marshall ran into a building's concrete.

He learned his lesson when using his phone:
Facebook and texting are best left at home.

DEAR RIVER PHOENIX

Laura Gabrion

Dear River Phoenix,
So full of hope
You proclaimed a life
Of good intentions,
But your Godly childhood
Succumbed to your confused adulthood
On Devil's night.
Instead of following your conscience,
You took that walk on the wild side of fate.
A ball of speed hurtling your short life
To a close,
And now you can no longer
Stand by me.

A distraught fan in Chicago

T1, T2

Laura Gabrion

To: lgabrion@hotmail.com
Hi! …got your name… from Patti…run leg…triathlon.

From: lgabrion@hotmail.com
…great…what's the distance?

To: lgabrion@hotmail.com
6.6 miles…meet on Sunday at 6:10 a.m. …my porch.

Sunday morning, the porch is cool and quiet,
What have I gotten myself into?
Amanda, who has lived half my life,
Is Speedo-ready to swim the Olympic distance.
Ann's lean bike, attached to her aging Suburban, shows signs of speed.

Sheepish conversations belie our disconnections.
What if I fail this group?
The black, waxy marker encodes us;
We make our way to the start.
An earsplitting blast of the airhorn sends the men first.

Minutes later another airhorn belch releases the women.
Chip velcroed to her slender ankle,
Amanda's arms cut through the open water
As the sun glints off MacArthur Bridge.
Oh my God! Amanda's catching up to the men!

She evenly strides to the shallow water
And runs through the seaweed-strewn sand.
Go! Go!

Ann moves expectantly to T1, awaiting the exchange;
The chip moves deftly from one ankle to the other.

Nerves swim from my stomach to my throat.
Where do I go?
Running across Belle Isle, the transition area, marked by the inflated T2,
Beckons those designated for the final stretch.
The nerves won't go back down to my stomach.

Stretching, sitting, standing, swallowing,
I wait. The girl next to me quips, "Can you run that far?"
Wry smile, nodding, I wait.
Where's Ann?
On cue, she wheels into the area, running alongside her bike.

My turn…fumbling, dropping, I secure the chip.
"Go! Go!"
The black asphalt radiates heat
As I scurry, single file, toward the cool dampness
Of the woods; *I can't get by…I need to get by.*

I reach for water; the half-filled cup
Spills to the ground.
No time…keep running.
I'm thirsty. I'm hot.
Keep running.

The balloons shift back and forth in the breeze, bordering the sign:
FINISH. Over the little bridge, up onto the asphalt and then grass,
I push. *Finish strong!*
Waving her arms, Ann screams:
"You did it!"

| **From**: lgabrion@hotmail.com |
| …hi…how'd we do? |

17

To: lgabrion@hotmail.com

…you'll never believe it…we won!

WHERE I AM FROM

Kim Grusecki

I am from Casimere and Elizabeth
from Schornak's IGA and the apartment above the store.
I am from the second kitchen with a flour-dusted kneading table,
an old worn comfy chair and a wringer washer near the wash tubs
(where all the babies were bathed).

I am from the high-peaked roof top well above the store.
From the wash that was hung out carefully, stories spun in exaggeration
and
children on their backs for hours and hours looking for the Big Dipper
and watching for shooting stars.

I am from pickled bologna served straight out of the barrel with
buttered Saltine crackers.
From Limburger cheese, sardines with vinegar and pills washed down
with creamed coffee slurped from a saucer whilst gagging and choking
them down.

I am from Four Roses whiskey, Pinochle games played until the wee
hours of the morning, Buicks and jokes told in Polish so the kids
wouldn't be able to understand.

I am from bread made from scratch pumped and pummeled on the
kneading table at 4:00 a.m. in the morning.

I am from women who served in WWII, unfiltered tobacco smoke
hanging in the air, the smell of frying bacon(with its grease stored
cumulatively in a Mason jar inside the refrigerator door) and fresh pies
in the oven.

From childhood days, I have grown but none of this is gone because
IGA stores, high peaked roofs, pickled bologna and frying bacon
always remind me of who I am and the two dear grocers from whence
I came!

THIS OLD PAIR

Kim Grusecki

In this old pair, the signs of age are showing. No matter how much I've cared for them, I'll have to let them go.

The outward signs are all there: creasing, cracking, wrinkling and thinning. The firmness of youth is gone – all indicators that time has taken its toll.

Sadly, our relationship is coming to an end, and I will have to do without them somehow. But how? They've been an important part of my life.

This pair has walked me through difficult days. They've covered me. They've protected me from the rain and cold and cushioned the strides I've made in life keeping me from many a fall.

I can't just leave them or put them in a home. I can't save them from this fate or discard them like most of the aged ones in our society.

So, I am searching for a resting place that will be their final abode. It must be a living, breathing tribute filled with other ancestral soles.

This old pair deserves a sacred burial ground not too far away. Where one removes their

shoes in respect and offers them up to pray.

A Mommy's Wish

Casey Joss

If I could give you one thing,
I would give you my arms to wrap around you in times of need and sadness.

If I could give you one thing,
I would give you a light that never burns out.

If I could give you one thing,
I would give you the curiosity to explore the world around you.

If I could give you one thing,
I would give you the courage to stand up for what you believe in.

If I could give you one thing,
I would give you the perseverance to follow your dreams.

If I could give you one thing,
I would give you laughter to make life less complicated.

If I could give you one thing,
I would give you comfort when you cry for mommy.

If I could give you one thing,
I would give you the confidence to always be yourself.

If I could give you one thing,
I would teach you not to be judgmental and critical of others.

If I could give you one thing,
I would give you the strength to keep going when the world is cruel.

If I could give you one thing,
I would give you dreams and aspirations beyond your wildest expectations.

My precious Bradyn and Bella: If I could give you one thing,
I would give you the world.

I love you,
Mommy

PURSE WARS

Casey Joss

A little tired of being used and abused,
Tossed into your closet, I'm a little confused
What's wrong with my soft, zebra skin?
Are you looking for someone a little more thin?

Apparently you only see me as your bar whore.
A romantic, quiet dinner is what I long for.

I'm rather elegant, unique, and beautiful.
But, club after club I stay dutiful.

I am very versatile.
You would see if you changed it up once in a while.

I am your purse, reserved for party nights with Jeff.
All that thumping music is making me go deaf.

I am begging you *PLEASE*,
Stop using me as your bar tease!

CYBER SONNET

Kathleen Reddy-Butkovich

I am a ghost: a voice without a face,
A spirit watching you behind a screen.
I'm waiting to be noticed in this place--
Now following through wires to be seen.
I ask the pedagogically hip
Are these the only characters you need?
I wonder if they see without a clip
Attached. Abandon notebooks! Write with speed!
But these keys unlock a melancholy;
For some still long for human talk and touch
And need a break from this solitary.
Yet there is risk if one resists too much.
    I will stall no more with this backward glance,
    I'll twitter with the best. I'll take the chance.

IN THE STILLNESS, BEYOND HUNGER

Kathleen Reddy-Butkovich

She reads his letter. The shape
of words in her mouth,
the shy pulse of hand
pushes through.
When gasping slows to a breath,
matters will change. I suspect.

Does the sponge caught in coral
feel the press of living things?
Lowly life form, full of acid rain,
wanting holy water.
The toss of ocean
shakes you, and you are free.
Does the house cat with claws
disguise infant cries on doorsteps?
Listen for the brass lid to lift.
You can
slip out with the mail
for a narrow escape.
There is a double vision now,
an exhaustion of eye contact.
The words leap and slant—
she can't unturn the page.
Will she survive, remain faithful,
keeping this one souvenir?

THE ANSWER

Pam Ryder

I need an education
but tuition is beyond my reach.
Working would raise the money
pushing graduation on.

Someone came to speak to us
the solution soon became apparent
Schooling could be free to me
if four years service I could give.

The family this man spoke of
different from my at home
A brotherhood uniting all who join
this elitist group.

We'd face our greatest challenge
stare down our fears together
Gaining mental, moral, physical strength
knowing failure's not an option.

Core Values will be taught and learned:
moral, ethical responsibility
Courage to overcome the worst,
a lifetime commitment to the corps.

I'll need to think less of myself
by putting others first
I'll find a sense of duty
to honor and defend.

For over 230 years
these warriors were "first to fight".
I want to be one of them, too.
The Marines. The Proud. The Few.

THE BADLANDS

Sara Vaughn

Cragged and rugged fists punch through the mist.
The waves of scarlet, amber, and lilac spread throughout the spires
Until the bright sunlight causes the colors to fade and languish.
I stand in awe at the hostile ground before me.
The islands of prairie grass whisper whimsical salutations to greet the
day.
I push my toes to the edge of the peak, peering down to the spectacle
below.
I stare forward following the path of the careening, screeching hawk.
His emotive cry echoing off the stone walls, until he veers into the sky
Leaving behind his ghost to mingle with the shadows of the Badlands.
The wind takes my breath rolling it over the jagged edges
Futile and weak.
Who am I against the vastness? Who am I in the greatness of this
land?
I inch closer, my toes dipping over the edge.

Wounded Knee

Sara Vaughn

The green sign wavers in front of me,
I look up at the hills surrounding me
And I wonder...

What would it be like to be here on that cold December night?
To have surrendered your way of life, your freedom, your rights
To be flying the white flag of peace outside of your tent
And to know that the Hotchkiss guns are waiting.

What would it be like to have to trust the people that were forcing you
from your lands?
Their greed for gold and lust for land forcing you out, making you
surrender,
Sending you away from the Black Hills and the Lakota,
Making it illegal to practice your faith.

What would it have been like to be sleeping peacefully and then be
swept into hell?
To have Black Coyote, deaf and unable to hear the order to surrender
all weapons
Accidentally fire a shot.
A shot that changed that night, changed everything.

What would it have been like to be sleeping with your children, trying
to stay warm?
To hear that single shot.
To hear the returning volley from the 7th Calvary
To go outside and see the battle below.
To see your husband, your sons, your friends slaughtered.

What would it have been like to hear the Hotchkiss guns firing
Not on the men fighting but on you and your children?
Turning to run, screaming in terror, you join the masses fleeing from
the encampment.

Why aren't the guns stopping? Why are they still firing?

What would it have been like to be huddled in the woods, hiding from the soldiers looking for you?
To see the clouds roll over the moon and the snow begin to fall.
To feel the temperature drop and your joints stiffen.
To drop your head against the ground and sleep.

What would it have been like on December 30th to see the bodies scattered and frozen?
To see the enemy dump the bodies into one grave, ignoring your customs and beliefs
To not be able to say good-bye and to just walk away from the giant hole in the ground
Where everyone, even your Chief, was thrown.

I walk over to the mass grave.
One marker surrounded by a chain link fence.
The gate is open, but I cannot force myself to walk inside.
Tears scald tracks into my cheeks and I look down in the dirt at my feet.
The anthill seems out of place in this place.
Mixed in among the ants, sand, and gravel,
The bright beads stand in stark contrast.
I stare at them as realization sinks in.
Ants always bring up what lies underneath.

I stare at the beads, tumbling around with the ants
And I wonder...

I AM FROM PITTSBURGH

Isabel Vukich

I am from Pittsburgh.
I am from yinz, hauscome, jeet jet, and redding up.
I am from three rivers that meet, valleys that flood,
and hills that bear inclines.
I am from steel mills, now razed,
replaced by parks and restaurants - hope for the future.
I am from a place where the weather is often
partly clah-dy an mahld.
I am from Isaly's chipped ham piled on sandwiches,
Iron City beer shared in beer gartens,
and galumbkes at every party in town.
I am from the neighborhoods of Mahnt Aver, Sahside, Lahrburl.
I am from an ethnic place, a cultural place, a quaint place,
but in many ways, a backward place.
I am from the home of Fred Rogers and Andy Warhol.
I am from the Cathedral of Learning where I was taught,
Carnegie Museum where I wondered,
and Kennywood Park where I kissed in the Old Mill.
I am from a town where people go food shoppin, meet dahnahahs,
and at the end of things - are laid aht.
I am from Picksburg, Pennsivania...
a place you can leave, but never leaves you.

CHAPTER 2

MEMOIRS

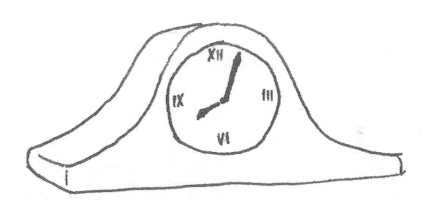

Act One: Could it Bee Betrayal?

Alexandra Adamus

Most people have a natural, healthy fear of bees, but not me. I guess I never felt I had any reason to dislike or fear the little guys. After all, they did bring us delicious honey, and helped keep things in balance in the environment. I've had plenty of exposure to bees over the years, but I had never been stung, so life was good. Actually, I kinda secretly believed somehow the bees and I had some sort of special relationship. I thought I understood them, and they understood me.

I spent many summers in Ontario, Canada, climbing a particular tree that grew freely in front of a honey house. Yes, there were plenty of bees resting peacefully on the tree, but I never feared them and would carefully climb over and around them as I made my way up the big tree. I never accidently squashed anyone, and I never got stung. On picnics, family gatherings, and camping trips there were always lots of bees. Other people would get up and fearfully move away. Not me--I wouldn't bother them, and they wouldn't bother me. We had a cooperative relationship with no need for any worry or adjustments to be made. We could simply, peacefully co-exist and enjoy a summer day. I really could not relate to other people's hysteria and fearful reactions to bees. That is until last summer.

One summer evening, I was supposed to be going to see my girlfriend's husband's band perform. Mind you, every time I would make a plan to go watch the band, something inevitability would get in the way. And so there I would be apologizing again, and again, and promising I would definitely be there next time. But not this time; I was determined that everything would go accordingly to plan. In fact, I had gotten ready to go extra early and now had time to kill. I was waiting around idly when I got the notion that perhaps I should use my time effectively and go pull a few weeds while I waited for my husband to finish getting ready.

I have a yard packed full of vegetation. Perennials and annuals grow wildly everywhere. It was on this day that I decided the side of the house needed some attention as it was quickly becoming overgrown with weeds. I started vigorously pulling out weeds one after another. "How had they got so out of control?" I thought to myself as I made my way deeper into the lush jungle. I was going at a nice pace, cutting back the brush, when I noticed a few insects hovering about. "Not a big deal," I thought as I wiped the sweat from my brow. I shooed away the pesky creatures. "Outta my way bugs! I have work to do!"

More weeds gave way, and I purposefully tossed them over my shoulder. A few more insects joined in the brigade. I squatted down and swished them away. "Onward, progress!" The cucumbers and tomatoes were looking relieved and finally able to breathe. I must've looked ridiculous; this weird lady dressed up to go out to a night club was out in the yard feverously pulling weeds with a cloud of angry insects hovering around the freshly sprayed hairdo that may have, coincidently, somewhat resembled a beehive.

It was at this point, when I had a huge clump of long grassy weeds in my hands and was squatted down and pulling with all my might, that all hell broke loose. All of the sudden the big patch of weeds came free, and I fell backwards and was suddenly dive bombed by a pack of angry bees! They attacked me from every angle. They were lodged in my hair, my eyes, my neck and arms, and one had attached itself to my lip and was hanging on for dear life. I had never felt such terrible, intense pain. I ran around in circles screaming," Help! Help!" I don't think I even fully realized what was going on. Somehow, I made my way into the house with several bees still attached. My husband, freshly out of the shower, helped me remove the remaining bees.

It didn't take long for the aftermath to settle in and show up on my face and body. My face suddenly swelled up like a flying zeppelin, and my lip became the size of a Mylar balloon. My whole body throbbed in pain. "Oh my God?! What happened?!" I asked.

"Looks to me like you just got stung by a swarm of bees," my husband replied.

"Bees? Are you sure?!" I asked in disbelief. I suddenly felt betrayed as my face continued to swell. I wondered if perhaps I should consider a visit to the emergency room. I decided I would rather die from anaphylactic shock than be stuck in a waiting room contemplating the co-pay charges that would surely follow. I opted out. I sat instead with cold rags and ice wrapped around my head, waiting for this to pass.

As my face and body began to take on a strange new shape, I realized I had to once again cancel on my friend. I felt weak. Besides,

I didn't think she would even believe me. Reluctantly, I picked up the phone and dialed.

"Anne?" I said through a small opening in my face. "I can't make it tonight."

"Oh?" I could hear silence on the other end.

"Yes, I'm sorry. I've been stung by a swarm of bees," I replied.

"Really?" she answered. I could hear the disbelief in her voice.

"Yes," I said.

"Okay, well…ah, I hope you feel better, and you really oughta' go to the hospital, you know," she said unemotionally as she hung up the phone.

Perhaps, I should have just gone to the club to prove to her that I really had been attacked by a bunch of angry bees, but I didn't feel so well. Maybe I really should just go the hospital. No, I figured at this point I would either die very shortly, or I would be making a full recovery. So, I just lay on the sofa and moaned quietly to myself.

Later that night, I went back outside to the scene of the accident to investigate. Yep, they were still there swarming and hovering around the place where I had pulled out the enormous clump of weeds. They were as mad as hell. I couldn't blame them; I had ripped away part of their home, and they clearly felt threatened. This time I decided to stay a respectful distance away. I wasn't taking any chances. The curious thing was their hive appeared to be in the ground. I made a note to myself to look it up later.

For days, friends stopped by to see the aftermath, and I would proudly walk them out to the sight like a tour guide and show them where it all happened. Everyone had an opinion and offered lots of advice on how to rid the territory of the bees. I decided to just let them be, and to my dismay my neighbor reported to me, days later, that she had exterminated them all, and I would be safe. I felt sad. For weeks I continued to feel somehow the bees had, perhaps, betrayed me, and I had also, perhaps, betrayed my best friend Anne.

WET AND WILD

Paticia Bieber

Phyllis is my best friend and worst enemy all rolled into one. She has these scathingly brilliant ideas that suck me in like diet-Pepsi up a straw. This one was no different. Her ideas always included three things: extensive strategic planning, many things to pack and danger to life and limb; usually mine. We were going to take a three day canoe trip down the Au Sable River! The "we" being Phyllis, her husband, John, and her son, Bill; my husband, Paul, myself, and our two sons, Tony and Chris.

Phyllis and I began this auspicious expedition by making lists, tons of them. Believe you me, Santa had nothing on us! We made them, checked them, revised them, and everything else in between. We listed tents, food, TP (toilet paper), bug spray, cooking utensils, charcoal, even a portable toilet seat, just in case. Everything was double-bagged in big, black, Hefty garbage bags. We weren't taking any chances!

Finally, C-Day arrived. Phyllis, true to form, supervised packing and loading operations like General Patton orchestrating the landing on Normandy Beach. Nothing got past Old Eagle Eyes. Of course, the last to be loaded were the troops. Needless to say, seating in the van was a little tight, so Tony had to sit on my lap. No problem! We were going to have the time of our lives; meeting each and every challenge that river could throw at us. Au Sable River, here we come!

I had never canoed before, but was assured that canoeing was easy; sort of like learning to ride a two-wheeled bike. I remember the learning-to-ride part was simple. It was the learning-to-brake part that was painful. I'd just ride down the street until I was even with the picker bushes in front of a house down the street and then just fall over. The bushes broke my fall and stopped the bike. Mission accomplished! It was painful, but "no pain, no gain!" Unfortunately, little did I know that the Au Sable was to become my picker bush.

We arrived at the canoe launch just as the sun was coming up, sleepy, but ready to begin our adventure. After a mini-lesson about canoe safety and procedure, we unloaded our cargo and stacked it down by the river. I remember the looks on the faces of the three guys who were assigned to load our canoes. They glanced at the pile of assorted items to be loaded into the canoes and asked incredulously, "Are you sure you want us to load all this stuff?" To which Phyllis promptly responded, "Of course." They rolled their eyes and shook their heads. I'm pretty sure they were making bets as to how long we would be on the river before they got a distress call to come rescue us. The canoe was sitting a little low in the water. Okay! More than a little!

Phyll and I had already decided that she would steer and I would paddle. Just to be clear, the person who steers sits in the back of the canoe and the person who paddles sits in the front. We boarded the canoe, sat in our assigned places, and promptly launched ourselves into the opposite bank, bounced off of it like a cue ball off the side of a pool table, and headed downstream, backwards. Eventually we did right ourselves, but little did I know that this was a foreshadowing of impending disaster.

Things went fairly well until we rounded a bend and came up on a huge tree whose limbs arched over the river. One of these limbs was home to a teeny, tiny black spider. At this point, I should probably tell you that Phyllis is inexplicably, unexplainably terrified of arachnids. For someone who jumps out of airplanes, scuba-dives regularly, and drives a race car, her fear of spiders is a mystery to me.

As we maneuvered the canoe under the limb, I saw the spider and prayed that Phyllis wouldn't. However, that was not meant to be. Suddenly, Phyll saw the spider. She started screaming like a banshee, reared up like a grizzly bear on its hind legs, wielded her oar like a samurai sword, and started pounding the limb like a butcher tenderizing a chunk of meat. That little spider didn't have a prayer. I'm sure he was dispatched post haste to that great spider web in the sky. May he rest in peace.

You have to be careful when you stand up in a canoe. As Phyllis stood, the canoe started rocking violently from side to side, heaving and pitching like a would-be bronco rider on a mechanical bull. I was thrown into the water and sunk like a stone. Fighting my way to the surface for air, I took a breath. I kept trying to right myself, but the stones, worn river-smooth, kept me slipping and sliding, battling to stay upright. Meanwhile, Phyllis was still in the canoe, dry as a bone, laughing hysterically and trying to paddle over to rescue me. With friends like her, who needs enemies? The water was only waist deep, so I gingerly made my way to the nearest bank. Phyll reached me and hopped into the water. We steadied the canoe and grabbed our floating cargo. However, there was a good ten inches of water in the bottom of the canoe. We needed something to bail out the canoe; something pail-like. Aha! I spotted two styrofoam cups lodged in the cattails that grew along the river. Phyll and I began to bail out the canoe. Suddenly, we heard a shout from down river. John and Paul had realized we weren't behind them and were fighting the current, paddling back to see if we were okay. They took one look at the two of us bailing out the canoe using styrofoam cups and dissolved into gales of laughter. I knew, at that point, Phyll and I would never live this one down!

John and Paul picked up the canoe, dumped out the water and helped us repack it. Hauling ourselves back into the canoe, undaunted but sopping wet, Phyll and I continued paddling downstream.

This was not the end, however, to my misery. It wasn't enough that my jeans, sweatshirt and unmentionables were sopping wet, but word of our troubles had spread downstream to my darling, considerate off-spring. We paddled past Bill and my sons, Tony and Chris. Do I hear, "Mom, are you all right?" Or, "Mom, are you hurt?" No! In typical Chris-like fashion, he yells, "Mom, are the Twinkies okay?" In the immortal words of Rodney Dangerfield, "I can't get no respect!"

The rest of the trip was a blast with only a few tiny little problems like stinky outhouses and forgetting to pack a can opener. Opening cans with an axe can be hazardous to your health! Phyll and I developed a rhythm to our paddling and pulled ahead of everyone else. It was so peaceful on the river. The animals seemed to emerge from the woods along the river's bank to say hello and wish us well.

After three days of canoeing and camping, we were to be picked up and driven by car back to the canoe launch site. Phyll and I arrived at the pick-up site first. While we waited for the other canoes to pull in, we talked about all the priceless memories we had made. I don't believe, I've ever laughed so hard or felt so close to a friend in my life.

Phyll and I are still best friends, soul-mates if you will. Since then, we have climbed Klingman's Dome, a mountain in Tennessee, and white-water rafted down the Youghiogheny River in Pennsylvania. Those stories, however, are for another time.

CONVERSATIONS WITH SATAN

Matthew Brown

Deanna Seifert spent the night at her friend Lindsay McCracken's house the same night Justin Lyons and I pitched a tent in his backyard and camped. The next morning, we woke up to the teeth of a city chainsaw cutting his tree down in the front yard. It had been struck by lightning. His mother had left that morning for work, and we walked into the front yard into a crowd of city workers with their stubble and their coffee. Justin asked them what they were doing, and they swore at him. 5 miles away, Deanna Seifert was no longer in Lindsay's bedroom. She was taken in the middle of the night by Andy Trombley, thrown in an old, beat-up van painted with grey primer probably around the same time we were making jokes about *Twin Peaks* and X-Men's "X-Cutioner's Song" storyline, which was wildly popular at the time. We tied a flashlight to the top of the tent; I would swing it around, contort my face into wickedness and say something about Laura Palmer. Justin would stop me.

Nobody stopped Andy Trombley. He went to the McCracken house around 2:00 am looking to abduct Lindsay. Trombley was upset with the McCrackens and wanted to take revenge by abducting their youngest daughter. Turns out, he got the wrong girl.

This was the summer after my fourth grade year, and the story didn't resolve itself until the end of July. Suburban Detroit parents turned on their television sets and panicked, listening intently to Bill Bonds deliver the latest news on little Deanna, locking their kids up at night, installing security systems, and checking their children by the hour. We were instructed again and again not to talk to strangers, and we unconsciously watched every car drive down the street with blank, questioning eyes, like a post-modern *Village of the Damned*. We would silently judge the most docile and polite strangers; kindly old men who reminded us of the friendly pharmacist from the Perry Drug commercials transformed into the sinister and perverted Gordon Jump from *Diff'rent Strokes*' "The Bicycle Man." How did that guy's career ever recover, anyways? I'll never buy a Maytag. Ever.

Justin's mom yelled at us for not calling her when the men came to cut the tree down. What were we supposed to do, become human shields? She worked all the time. That's why we were at Justin's a lot.

We spent that whole summer either at Justin's or at my house, in my pool. I remember making up new dives off the board and feeling the raw, scorched backs that came with attempting these gymnastic maneuvers. We thought that having materials between our skin and the water would alleviate the pain of a particularly horrible back-smacker. In a moment of pure genius, one of us suggested cutting holes in trash bags to wear around our bodies while swimming. We were five ten-year olds swimming around sleepily in a large in-ground pool with giant plastic garbage bags dancing around our faces, tempting fate. Paul Walsh used to skateboard off of the slide into the pool. We thought this was hysterical, oblivious. One day, Alan Yubanski swam under the Fun Island in the middle of the pool and didn't come out for a long time. We happily splashed around for a full minute-and-a-half in our plastic death-vests before I noticed weak air bubbles popping up under the heavy inflatable island that took up eighty percent of the deep end. Alan barely made it. Pool safety wasn't our strong suit.

As the Seifert story grew into its second month, we sat in Justin's basement with a Ouija board. I'd never used a Ouija board before and felt like I shouldn't. To me and my Sunday school upbringing, Ouija boards represented the pinnacle of evil, a manifestation of supreme horror sitting on a shelf next to *Monopoly* and *Risk*. Didn't feel like playing the game of *LIFE*? Not in the mood for *Stratego*? Nothing says "kid-friendly" like a spiritual gateway to contact the undead. I mean, *Sorry*'s great and all, but with a Ouija board, you don't even need other friends to play with! It can just be you and the spirits. This is an especially fun game if you enjoy crippling nightmares and bed-wetting.

Rory Garr gently poked fun at me, and I reluctantly conceded. I didn't want to do it. This was divination. I'm no sorcerer. This was somewhere in my life between the time that I ran home because my friends were playing with matches, and the time I stayed in another room while they watched a dirty movie. It was a moral, spiritual, and social grey area for me, so I went along with it because I was an idiot.

Rory, Justin, Alan, and I sat down around the Ouija board, turned off the lights, and went to work. First stop, Deanna Seifert. Justin attempted to summon her or the spirits who would know anything about her. I wanted to leave. This wasn't right, at all. The Ouija triangle started moving and speaking to us. It spelled out the answers to our fourth grade questions about Deanna Seifert, the girl who would have gone to our school and possibly shared our class, had we lived 3 mile roads south. We asked the spirit if Deanna was alive. The triangle moved to NO. She was dead. The girl whom we had heard about for weeks was dead, and nobody knew it but us. The killer probably knew too, we supposed. We asked where she was, and it spelled out "FACTORY." Justin asked it to be more specific. It then spelled out "TRASH." We deduced that she was in the dumpster of a factory somewhere in Warren, the little geniuses that we were.

Then something took the Ouija board over. The triangle started moving erratically all over the board. Who were we talking to? The Ouija board spelled out "SATIN," which was close enough to Satan for any of our comfort. Somehow, I knew this would happen and felt like I deserved it. What happens when you dabble in the occult? You get to know the Prince of Darkness. None of us were too keen to meet him after he started spelling out words we didn't even know were curse words. We quickly put the board back in its box (Justin claimed it was warm to the touch, which made me want to vomit), ran upstairs, and threw it under Justin's brother's bed, where he hid all of his pornography.

Having just spoken candidly with Satan, we decided the best course of action was to ride our bikes across the neighborhood and into the woods, as it seemed we were best protected there. We'd heard that Ouija boards couldn't be burned, and that Satan could possess your soul through one, and that your family could be haunted by what you had done. Rory mentioned *The Exorcist*, which set us hours behind in our attempt to stop thinking about the afternoon's madness. Eventually, we came to our senses and went our separate ways. When my parents asked me what I had done that day, I nervously lied to them.

A week later, Deanna Seifert was found in her nightgown in a metal bind behind a machine shop less than a mile away from the McCracken house where she had been abducted. Trombley realized he grabbed the wrong child and consequently beat her to death with a chunk of concrete. She was found in that dumpster less than two months later, littered with metal chips, her underwear inside out. Justin and I looked at each other silently, knowing that somehow, we were responsible, thinking that everything would have been okay had we not cosmically changed things with that Devil board, knowing that everything about our lives had changed with it.

We discussed the board. What would we do with it? My idea was to bury it in the woods, which was met with laughter and derision. As far as I know, it's still there, laying underneath Jeff's bed, pornography scattered amongst the medium in which I spoke with Lucifer. It seems like after that summer, it was forgotten, like the memory of that little girl to all of us.

As the years went on, bad things continued to happen. Children were abducted, people were murdered, parents divorced. Friends robbed each other, became violent, died. Alan, in a car with a woman twenty years his senior with whom he was romantically involved, died in an awful accident. Paul Walsh, the boy who taught me how to skateboard, was hit by a train, following the tracks home from a party, drunk. He survived, but he uses a cane and gives motivational speeches about alcohol abuse to high-schoolers. I saw him in the supermarket last week, and he didn't remember me.

The infant boy who would have been Deanna Seifert's nephew died in 2008 after being found in her younger brother's rat-infested home. The baby was addicted to drugs and cold.

I don't know if everyone else just forgot or what. Satan doesn't just leave you and possess a herd of pigs anymore. He sticks around, or at least he did with me. That afternoon in Justin's basement stayed with me long after the Seifert Murder Trial passed on into local media obscurity. All of these terrible things were because of me. I killed that girl. I was the reason. It wasn't Andrew Trombley or Lindsay McCracken or Satan, it was me. Had I just listened to the lessons I learned from *Parables of Nature* filmstrips as a child, had I just gone home, my fingers wouldn't have made that horrible contact with the devil. Deanna might have been found as a run-away. She might have gone to prom and kissed a boyfriend. She might have been a great aunt, steering her little brother away from drug addiction and child neglect, but these things were not to be. I had played my part. I was sure of it.

A few summers after our collective experience with Satan, Justin's older brother attempted suicide. We found him on his kitchen floor in a puddle of vomit. Justin called the ambulance. As I watched Jeff lie there and groan closer to death, all I could picture was the triangle with the glass in the center fly around that board, and the sharp, jolting movements of the devil's hands, coming to take us one-by-one. Rory told me years later that he had been moving the piece all along.

I'm still not sure I believe him.

"Niagara Falls"

Matthew Brown

I told my dad I was afraid I was going to hell. At five. I told him this at five years old. I sat on my mom and dad's bed and cried for hours. I should have been playing with action figures. I should have been outside, swimming. Instead, I thought about Sunday school, cigarette butts, and Lana Foster and how all of these things were leading me squarely into hell.

Earlier that day, I picked up a cigarette butt from the edge of my driveway. It'd probably been thrown there by Reggie or Bobby Jacks, the official neighborhood bullies. At 10, these boys bragged of drinking alcohol. By fifth grade, these cats were shaving. They were the kind of people that could beat up anyone, and often did. When I was little, I thought my dad could beat up anyone (most kids did), but I still thought Reggie and Bobby might give him some trouble. I made the mistake one time of saying the wrong thing to Reggie, Bobby, and their friend Billy Apples. This kid's name was Billy Apples. It sounded like something out of CandyLand. He didn't look like something out of CandyLand, though. I was riding my bike around the block when Billy Apples asked what I was looking at. Truth be told, they were stabbing the ground with knives, which repulsed and attracted me. It was hard not to look. When he asked what I was looking at, I responded with a weak "shut up," which was, in hindsight, not the best course of action. Reggie, Bobby, and Billy Apples chased me around the neighborhood for about twenty minutes with knives in hand. It was the longest chase of my life until I turned sixteen, and Kevin Vance chased me over fences and through yards in Warren for kissing his girlfriend, who was drunk on Ny-Quil, after a show. Somehow, I managed to outlast my pursuers in both chases.

I picked up the butt from the driveway. Lana was with me. I put the cigarette butt to my lips, cold, unlit, ridiculous. Doing my best Esai Morales from *La Bamba*, I sucked in gravel, Styrofoam, and (as I thought at the time) piles of cancer. Lana laughed, and I felt guilt (and most likely cancer) shoot through my body like the sudden shock and guilt of taking the Lord's name in vain and knowing it. I asked Lana to go home, and she did, crossing the street barefoot in a pink swimsuit, slamming her screen door, and being yelled at by her mother.

I walked into my house, into the bathroom, and I threw up. I hoped that the cancer was out of me, but at five, I knew this wasn't medically feasible. I could feel surging through my body, eating and destroying me from within, just like in *Alien*. All of this from a playful drag on a cigarette butt to impress Lana Foster. I was dying, and it was time to make peace with my Lord and my family.

I knew that confession and repentance were key. I hit my 2-year-old brother in the face with a couch cushion. Small and poorly balanced, he hit the basement floor and got a concussion. I threw a dart at my sister's stomach. It stuck in, and she looked up at me with a mixture of shock and betrayal, as if to say, "How could you, my own brother?" I "played doctor" with Lana in my basement with the lights off. We re-enacted scenes from *The Karate Kid Part II*, only without clothes on. Because of these things, and many others, I was going to hell. My dad looked at me with his hair that grew toward the sun (as my little sister put it) and read Matthew 19 out of an old, brown NIV Bible about Jesus and the little children. He gently convinced me that I wasn't going to hell.

"You don't have cancer either, Matthew."

A load was lifted off of me. I thought of him as Superman, saving me from falling off of the guard rail at Niagara Falls. I leaned in to kiss him.

"Brush your teeth."

"Tic-Tac"

Matthew Brown

My friend Mike passed a kidney stone in eighth grade. At school. We were in Dr. Kehling's class, and Mike asked for a pass to go to the bathroom. He was hunched over and looked as if he were in pain; he rushed out of the room, and we all listened intently, knowing that he was pretty sick. We heard the door of the bathroom slam shut. The next thing we heard was a dull, long scream, much like the sound of a tornado siren. We all knew that it was the sound of a 12 year-old boy shooting solidified chunks of mineral deposits through his urethra. The thing was, we thought it was hilarious. The class erupted in laughter.

This was the same kid who dislocated his knee 4 years later in gym class. He went for a jump shot and landed on his knee wrong, and we looked at him as he lay on the freshly waxed floor with his kneecap somewhere where it definitely shouldn't have been. He started screaming much like the scream that came from the men's room at Reed Junior High. The gym teacher came over and started asking him if he was alright. Mike responded with a string of profanities that we had never heard before. He said words that were absolutely unfamiliar to us. As we looked on, it started again. We were losing control, laughing hysterically at the scene we were witnessing. Mike had just cursed our gym teacher out so bad that he deserved to be expelled, as statements like "are you okay" aren't usually followed with "I'll kill you where you f—king stand!" We protected ourselves by laughing, unaware or fully aware of the tremendous pain our friend was in.

The next year, I was sitting in Mr. Kurrault's physics class with Mike. Mike and I were waxing philosophically about the strange fact that the great American writer Mark Twain's name rhymed with cocaine; Mike thought that this was hysterical. He thought it was even more hysterical when I pointed out that the same was true of local sportscaster Don Shane. Mike sat there in starry disbelief, as if the cosmos had just been revealed to him. He may have been high. I'm not sure. Regardless of what his mental state was, what happened next is not disputed—I suffered through the worst physical pain I had ever experienced in my very brief life. Within a matter of seconds, a Tic-Tac found itself lodged inside my nasal cavity.

In order to explain how this happened, it's necessary to backtrack a little bit. So, I used to throw up. All the time. We're talking day after day. Remember the kid who threw up every day in elementary school? I was that kid. Truth be told, a major portion of my adolescence was spent throwing up, which I would do if anything occurred that was just outside the realm of normalcy. For your reading pleasure, here is a list of things that actually made me throw up before the age of 13:

Talking to girls
Talking to teachers
Talking to friends
When my sandwich was NOT bologna and cheese
When I could not climb the rope
When others threw up
When others belched in my face (this continued well into high school)
When I peed my pants in 2nd grade
Throwing up 5 minutes prior
Math Tests
Leaving home
Too much chocolate milk
Not enough chocolate milk
Large Marge from *Pee Wee's Big Adventure*
Christmas (thinking I saw Santa Claus)
The stench of owl pellets
Sexual education films
7th Grade

The problem was that I kept throwing up. Even in high school, I struggled from a wicked nervous stomach. I was a nervous guy, no kidding. I'd get real anxious and worked up, and the only release was a physical one, namely of the vomit variety. Turns out, throwing up in public at the age of eighteen leads people to believe that you're drunk or dying. So, in order to avoid this social stigma, I chewed stuff: breath mints, Swedish Fish, chewing gum, anything really. It eased my nerves and calmed my stomach, and there were honestly times when it was the only thing that kept me from spilling my stomach's contents everywhere.

One time, I threw up getting out of the car in the parking lot at Cedar Point. I went down with friends and was planning on meeting a girl I was trying to date there. I threw up all over the side of the car. I didn't even make it to the rides.

I threw up before Senior Prom and busted the blood vessels in my face, giving myself two incredibly handsome black eyes. I really wanted my girlfriend to have a nice time, and I worked myself up about it so much that I vomited in the shower. My face looked like raw meat, purple and white, like a Good-and-Plenty box. I wore sunglasses to prom and felt like the epitome of douche-baggery. You see, people who wear sunglasses indoors are stupid idiots. People who wear sunglasses indoors to hide a disaster area of a face are no better. So, like I said, I chewed on stuff quite often. There's a picture of me at prom, looking like Robert Smith, with my favorite teacher from high school. I'm smiling pretty big in the picture, and you can see a Breath Saver in the corner of my mouth. I was a mess.

So, back in Mr. Kurrault's class, when Mike made that incredible remark about Don Shane, Mark Twain, and cocaine, I laughed, paying no attention to the wintergreen Tic-Tac that was in my mouth (note the flavor; this is important to our story). Accordingly, I found that the Tic-Tac made its way down my esophagus during a sharp intake of breath whilst laughing.

Getting things down your windpipe is not a good idea. My mom used to have this habit of sticking a Life-Saver in between her front teeth and sucking air through it, until her teeth lost their grip and the candy went hurtling down her throat, lodging itself about 4 inches down. It was actually kind of funny because every time she said anything or breathed, she started whistling, because of the hole in the center. That being said, when something goes down your throat, your instinctual reaction is to bring it back up. Usually one can do this by coughing. This was the course of action that my body planned on taking after the Tic-Tac began its journey. I did my best to cough it up, hoping that I would spit it out and not throw up.

Unfortunately, God and this Tic-Tac had other plans. Instead of coughing up and exiting out my mouth, the Tic-Tac missed the turn and took a detour through my nasal passages, finally coming to rest about five centimeters up my nose.

At first, I have to admit that I was relieved. Compared with coughing something up, which posed a great risk of throwing up to our intrepid hero, digging something out of my nose was much, much easier. Sure, maybe a little socially irresponsible, but nonetheless, I was glad. However, it quickly became apparent that the Tic-Tac wasn't going to come out of my nose so easily, as every finger of mine proved to be too large for my nasal orifice. I asked Mike for help, but he didn't want to stick any of his much more feminine fingers up my nose either. On a side note, he was born with an auxiliary thumb that wasn't removed until the age of five. That is incredibly funny. My wife told me this part is extraneous. So was that thumb. I'll remove it five years from now.

So, here I was, Tic-Tac lodged up my nose. This was when I started panicking. I tried blowing it out like a snot rocket. Nothing. I tried sucking and snorting it back in, hoping that it would somehow end back up in my mouth. Again, it was not moving. I actually resorted to punching myself in the face trying to dislodge it. None of this worked. After about a minute of solutions that didn't work, Mike suggested that the only way it was coming out was by melting down. Unfortunately, he was right. A brief interlude of time passed, a section that I now refer to as the calm before the storm, and suddenly, every orifice of my face started pouring water. Water came streaming from my eyes, my mouth, and gushing out of my nose. The floodgates opened, and God screamed at me to stop being stupid. That's when I was smote by his wrath.

I can't begin to describe the searing pain that was coming from my face. It's as if a thousand suns ignited inside my nose and told me they hated my guts. These weren't just dying stars; these were yellow and red giants with a personal vendetta against me. From that day forward, I felt a kindred bond with Ghost Rider, since I also knew what it felt like to have my head engulfed in flames. Here's the thing about the water that was coursing out of my face: it wasn't at all quenching my pain. In fact, it was making it much worse. It was salty and horrible, and I swear to God it tasted like mint. I was crying wintergreen tears. If it wasn't so horrible, certain countries would consider this a miracle.

I don't remember any other student being in that class other than me and Mike. Mr. Kurrault sent me to the office—I had to be escorted because I couldn't see. My mom kept telling me to dump my head in water, which made things worse, I'm pretty sure. From the time I got home, it took the Tic-Tac about twenty minutes to burn off, which pretty much felt like sucking water up your nose for twenty minutes straight, only instead of water, it was like sucking burning coals—burning coals with bees on them. And the bees had swords. And the swords had tiny little ninja stars with Tic-Tacs attached to each point. That's pretty much what it was like. I remember a horrible, minty-fresh post-nasal drip. I had an epically sore throat for about two weeks.

A few years ago, I had an ulcer and doctors had to send a camera down my throat to look in my stomach. They were going to put me under, knowing my weak stomach. Unfortunately, they didn't pump me full of enough anesthetic. I woke up when the tube started sliding down my throat and proceeded to try and pull it out. They quickly put me back to sleep and finished the procedure. My mom asked me if it was worse than the Tic-Tac.

Truth is, it didn't even compare. Waking up in the middle of having something jammed down your throat was scary, and I lost some sleep, but the Tic-Tac changed my life. For starters, I never put anything in my mouth that will fit in my nose. Ever.

I tell this story to each of my high school classes as a cautionary tale. A couple years ago, one of my classes presented me with a gift pack of Tic-Tacs as a birthday gift. I gave them away an hour later. They also got me Sea-Monkeys. I accidentally killed them all when I ran out of food and fed them the rest of my bagel. I thought everybody liked bagels.

CHICAGO – 1993

Laura Gabrion

I am a daddy's girl, so the fact that I am a marathoner is surprising to no one in my immediate family. As a young girl, I watched my dad run past our front porch in his Bruce Jenner shoes and cut-off shorts. Offering to be helpful, my sister and I set up Dixie Riddle cups filled with water. Not long after that, I tried desperately to follow him around the perimeter of our neighborhood. I'd make it a block or two, and then I would peter out. After a few months, I got the clever idea to run in the opposite direction; in crossing, I would shout a few things at my dad looking to merely make a connection. As it was, it would be many years before I could run easily next to my dad. Some people spoke of the new-fangled microwave ovens and Betamax video recorders, but in our house, we heard my dad speak of such things as Bill Rodgers, Frank Shorter, Gortex, and the almighty—the Boston Marathon. In the 70s, a qualifying time for this race for a 40 year old male was a 3:10 marathon, which means running at a 7:15/mile pace for 26.2 miles. My dad pushed diligently for many years, but that goal was such a difficult one. While he came close, the Big One eluded him. He unforeseeably passed that torch on to me.

When my husband Doug and I moved to Chicago and began graduate school, a friend from home moved into our condo with us. One snowy February day, Mark threw out an offer. "You want to train for Chicago with me?" I worked full-time and went to school at night, but some part of me felt compelled to reply, "Sure! That sounds great!" Most people do not train for a single race for seven months, but Mark and I got out every day and ran. Even when he moved, we would meet in a central location and run whatever the daily schedule called for. I went from ten miles to fifteen miles to twenty miles. I truly could not believe that I was doing this! Sincerely, I had always enjoyed a leisurely jog, but I never thought I would have the stamina to run this far. My self-pride grew with the miles, and my graduate school classmates called me "The Runner." Having been the least athletic person…you know, the last one picked for teams and the first one pegged in the head with a dodge ball…this was a twist.

The weekend of the race finally came. It was October 31, 1993, and my parents had come in the night before. My dad planned on running as much of the race with me as possible. He would run the first ten miles, and then he would cut across the city at the 10 mile mark so that he could pick me up again at the 20 mile mark. We set our clothes out the night before. My number was pinned carefully to my shirt, and my shoes and socks were on the kitchen counter. Next to my stuff lay my dad's. We were ready to go. Sunday morning, we woke up to an inch of snow on the ground, and River Phoenix had died during the course of the night after overdosing on a speedball at the Viper Room. This was not a good sign. I had a tendency to perseverate on such tragedies—Princess Diana's death four years later nearly landed me with a prescription for Prozac. I took one look out the window and told my dad quite plainly, "Look, Dad, I can't run this thing. There's snow on the ground, and besides, River Phoenix died last night."

"Who?" My dad sipped his coffee and looked at me for a minute. "Laura, you can do this. It will be hard, but you can do it. Get your stuff on."

Grudgingly, I complied. I dressed myself cautiously and applied Vaseline liberally. When you run for more than three hours, everything begins to rub against you. In those days, Vaseline made it bearable; today's products are much less gooey. The race started at 7:30 a.m., so Mark arrived a little after 6:00 a.m. Our plan was to have Doug drive us down and drop us off; he, my mom and my sister would meet us at the end.

It was a cold and gray Chicago morning when my dad, Mark and I got out of the car. We said our good-byes to my husband, and he wished us luck. He knew I was on the edge, so he got out of there quickly! Mark, my dad, and I were planning to start together, but prerace jitters set in, and I had to find a bathroom. There was a church on the corner of Washington and Clark, so we went in. Unbelievably, the church had two exits. My dad and I went out of the one on Washington, and Mark went out of the one on Clark. I didn't have any time to contemplate it. There were over 20,000 runners, and I was trying to find a place to jump in. The airhorn sounded, and we were off. Mark had a hideous yellow shirt on, so I thought for sure I would find him. In fact, I didn't find him until about the fifth mile of the race.

My dad and I ran at a comfortable pace until we caught up to Mark. We ran together for a few more miles, and then my dad broke away so he could find me again at the 20 mile mark. I had trained for so many months with Mark, but around the 15th mile, things started to get a little crazy for me. I am a firm believer in the concept of "mind over matter," but I couldn't get my head around the fact that I still had eleven miles to go. I was cold, my feet hurt, and that River Phoenix thing was still bugging me. Mark did the best thing he could do at that point—he bailed on me and pulled ahead. It was better for him, but it was worse for me. Each mile I kept a repetitive statement rolling through my mind: "Five more miles to Dad. Four more miles to Dad..." I was oblivious to running through the neighborhoods of Chicago. I just wanted to see my dad.

Mile 20. The Monroe Harbor was on the right, and the northern edge of Grant Park was on the left. A majority of the spectators were in this area because they could stand in one spot and see a person cross at 20 and again at 25. My eyes darted furtively back and forth on either side of the road. Where was my dad? Suddenly, he fell in beside me. "Daddy," I groaned. I hadn't called him that in at least fifteen years. "I am done. Let's quit."

"Oh no you don't! You're not quitting now. You're almost done."

"Dad, I have six miles to go."

"We'll do it. Together."

I was too tired to fight him. I listened to the cadence of his voice, and it took my mind off of my thirst, my fatigue, and my aching feet. We ran north past the Drake Hotel, and we circled back and passed it again going south towards Grant Park. I knew that if I could simply cross the finish line, I could sit down or lie down or just be down. It really didn't matter at this point! At mile 25, my sister jumped in. She was wearing street shoes and a long, wool winter coat, but she was determined to help me finish.

"Gonna Fly Now" was wafting out of the speakers as we entered the final stretch. We passed my mom, who had been joined by my college roommate. They yelled out for me, and I smiled feebly. Would this race never end!?

We rounded Jackson, and I could see the rainbow of balloons. Like a crazed lunatic, I decided to sprint it in, and my poor sister in her Nine

West shoes had to follow suit. My dad moved to the other side of me, and I grabbed their hands. We crossed the finish line together, arms raised up in victory, and I announced, "I will never do this again."

It's funny how the mind works. With the healing strokes of time, any bit of pain can be forgotten. It has been fifteen years since that first marathon. On October 12 this year, I will run Chicago again for the first time since 1995. It will be my 20th marathon.

Men Are Like Purses

Casey Joss

Men are like purses. At least, that's the case in my household. It's taken me some time to catch on; I have been watching my sister hone this notion over the last year.

I watch her leave on nightly escapades. Her name is Taryne or, as my family jokingly calls her, "bar fly." Twenty-six and still looking for "the one." When she first moved in with me, I would have to ask her, "Who are you going out with tonight?" Now, after a year of quiet observation, no questions are required. You see, men are like purses. I can tell exactly who she will be spending her evening with by the purse she carries.

My sister would kill me if she knew of my hypothesis. She doesn't take kindly to the locker room talk the family has about her social life. I guess I can't blame her, but it sure is entertaining.

Here is some data that puts my speculation to the test:

Scott. I know she will be having dinner with Scott when she takes one of her expensive and more reserved bags. Scott is a bit older than she is and owns his own successful accounting firm. The purse matches the man; classy, not too loud, reserved. Scott usually gets a Coach or Kate Spade. Are you following me?

Jeff. He requires a more fun, trendy purse: brightly colored or animal print purses. Jeff is a party guy. They usually spend their nights dancing at the hottest new club.

Danny. A laid-back, outdoorsy guy, he calls for a canvas or straw handbag. Taryne and Danny have been skiing, rollerblading, and biking, to name a few dates. I think at one point I actually watched her leave with a camouflage bag; maybe they were going hunting?

Women like to change their purses. We change them according to our mood or the season. Taryne changes her purse according to the man in her life.

e-Baying by the Light of the Moon

Cornelia Pokrzywa

I have a secret vice. Throughout the day, between work and family obligations, I flip open my laptop, log on, scroll down and hold my breath. How much money have I made today? It's not the stock market or pork belly futures I'm tracking. An on-line auction, more specifically eBay, is my destination. Lots of people are addicted to on-line shopping, but I've become enthralled with the flip side – on-line selling. Nothing in our house is considered safe as I cast my roving eye for the next item going up for bid.

It all began a few years ago, when my husband handed me an article from a business publication about eBay, also known as the world's biggest garage sale. No item is too insignificant to sell on eBay. More surprisingly, virtually no item goes unsold. Old pairs of designer shoes, unused exercise equipment, musical instruments that never played a note in tune – you name it, and it's for sale on eBay.

We have an average, middle-class household, but a quick trip down to the basement revealed a kaleidoscopic collection of unneeded and unused – well, let's be honest – *junk*. The axiom that one man's trash is another man's treasure has never been truer – and the power of the Internet brings the individual who most desires your unwanted odds and ends close at hand. As an eBay newbie, I started by researching items I had that I suspected might be worth some money. Some Christmas-themed collector's plates I purchased on a whim during a college-student stint as a china shop associate turned out to be worth $250 each! I put them up for auction and giggled gleefully when the money magically appeared in my checking account just seven days later.

Noticing that designer handbags were a hot seller on the auction block, I sorted through my purse collection. There were four that I no longer carried, so after a quick digital photo shoot, they were up for bid. Not knowing what to expect, I opened the bidding at a mere $10 apiece. Lo and behold, seven days later my abused Kate Spade diaper bag fetched nearly $70. This was a bag that had been to hell and back – I have three children! – but even with a photograph showing visible stains and an honest description about its condition, 27 people bid like crazy for it. Infant and children's items are especially in demand on eBay. A quick glance through my daughters' closets turned up outgrown shoes, dresses, and even little miniature handbags. Perhaps the most surprising item to have value on eBay – believe it or not – is used cloth diapers! As a new mother, I had spent about $400 on plush, organic cotton to swaddle my babies' bottoms in a small attempt to help save space in landfills. Once they all graduated from my potty-training camp, I never expected to use the old cloth diapers for anything except rags – but that was before I discovered on-line auctioning. There were other new mothers out there who were even more committed to the environment than I was – they were willing to buy *used* cloth diapers for their babies' bottoms. I recouped half of my investment and gained a whole new perspective on recycling.

Pretty soon, the pile of items up for auction grew larger and the home office became a shipping company, strewn with boxes, padded envelopes and various packaging supplies. My husband, who initially guffawed at several of the items I put up for bid, quickly became helpful, weighing my packages on a specially-purchased fish-hook scale and sending them out promptly as the auctions ended. He joined me on my searches through the house – turning up forgotten knickknacks, cobwebby fitness equipment, and ignored toys. The question, "Are you using this?" took on an entirely new meaning for us.

We soon started speaking a new lingo. "This is NWT," I would remind my husband as he debated a starting price for an item. That stands for New with Tags. There are thousands of such items listed on eBay. Apparently, I'm not the only one who makes purchases she regrets. Or how about NWOT – that means you actually removed the tags, intending to use the item, but never did. There are thousands of those on eBay, too.

Like enthusiastic real estate agents, eBayers (as we like to call ourselves) describe items in code. "Gently worn in my smoke-free, pet-free home" is a popular description which calls to mind a woman lounging in a deodorized, hermetically-sealed glass house. "Shows signs of wear" is one to watch out for – it could mean anything from slight wrinkling to near destruction. Still, the vast majority of sellers are honest – and the system rewards those who get positive feedback from their customers with special tags and flags such as "PowerSeller." My seller ID features a green star, the number 408 to indicate completed transaction, and the coveted "100% Positive Feedback" which lets potential buyers know I've never cheated anyone.

Like traditional retailers, eBayers experience seasonal spikes in sales. For children's clothing, the best time of year is "BTS" (back-to-school) which runs from mid-July until late September. Predictably, the holiday season is equally brisk; unlike brick-and-mortar retailers, who *discount* heavily after the holidays, eBayers happily re-sell their unwanted gifts MIB (mint-in-box) at top dollar for a tidy profit. No more waiting in line at the mall to return Aunt Gladys' well-intentioned but poorly-conceived gift ideas. Since I began eBaying, my children have learned to open gifts very carefully, just in case it turns out to be something we don't want to keep.

Some people might think it's dishonest or ungrateful to re-sell gifts on eBay, but I disagree. Regifting has been around a lot longer than eBay, and besides, my family members all know about my predilection for auctions -- they choose gifts more wisely with this knowledge.

Like most children, my kids had hoarding instincts, and it took them a while to come around to seeing the benefits of eBay. "Where's Kit?" my nine-year old asked suspiciously when her American Girl Doll went missing. "Wherever you left her," I offered with a clear conscience, although we both knew that if Kit didn't start spending more time outside of the closet, her perpetual plastic grin was going to be beamed out over the Internet in a mug shot, with a description and a minimum starting bid. I realized the tide had turned when I snapped up a cute pair of Disney Crocs at Nordstrom only to have my youngest daughter turn her nose up at them. "I don't like them," she announced with a six-year-old's certainty. "But everybody likes Crocs," I insisted. "Put them on eBay," she replied. I know they must have absorbed a few urban legends about people making huge sales with Virgin Mary grilled cheese sandwiches and unusually-shaped cornflakes. When we picked strawberries this summer, my daughter's friend came out of the patch hiding a heart-shaped berry she planned to sell on eBay for $500.

I thought I would eventually run out of items to put up for auction. But growing children go through an astonishing quantity of clothes, toys, and equipment. I no longer feel guilty for replenishing my own closet with this year's trendy items as long as I auction off last year's trendy items. What could be better than getting cash for things that would otherwise collect dust in the basement? Without a doubt, the world's online marketplace is adding excitement and profit – and a little glimpse into human nature -- to my late nights in front of the laptop.

A Visit to the Place for Girls

Cornelia Pokrzywa

My husband and I recently decided to take our three young daughters on a visit to nearby Chicago, that quintessential Midwestern city teeming with museums and fun city life. We planned, researched and got tips from friends and relatives about the "must-see" sites. Without exception, everyone listed the world-class aquarium, the natural history museum, the planetarium and – because we have three daughters – everyone insisted we must make time for American Girl Place.

If you are acquainted with a young woman under the age of 12, then you already know about the American Girl phenomenon. Conceived in 1986, the American Girl brand is a fabulously successful direct marketer of historical fiction books and dolls which help young girls connect with our nation's past in a fun, positive way. None of this history comes cheap, though. Dolls start at $90 and you could easily spend more than $1000 to collect the entire line of accessories for any one doll. You could pay for a college education with the amount you'd spend to collect all the dolls and their accessories.

Still, I admired the Pleasant Company (now owned by Mattel) for creating and promoting this line of wholesome dolls. I didn't object to purchasing the truly beautiful Native American doll my oldest daughter requested one Christmas. We even sprung for several of "Kaya's" pricey accessories, like a $65 pony.

I knew a visit to American Girl Place wasn't going to come cheap, but not in my wildest dreams was I prepared for the reality I encountered in the prominent, three-story building located just off Chicago's famed "Magnificent Mile" of shopping. The windows featured large photos of wholesome, smiling girls. Various dolls peered out, posed in appealing attire amid the store's signature red star, a nod to the patriotic undertones of the brand, which aspires to offer something for every girl in America.

Reality check: Unless you belong to the upper-middle class, American Girl Place may as well slam its maroon double-doors right in your face.

Inside, I found a miniaturized version of any adult woman's dream shopping experience. Spacious, well-lit and sparkling, American Girl Place features hundreds of untouchable dolls perfectly posed behind glass display cases. This, you quickly realize, is not a toy store.

In fact, American Girl Place is a mini-department store, complete with a café, a photography studio and even a theatre which stages live musicals. Lunch in the café, which requires advance reservations, will set you back $20 per person. Many friends recommended having lunch, brunch, tea, or dinner in the café, which encourages guests to bring along their dolls and seats them in specially-designed chairs at each table. The food, I heard, was wonderful.

But I have three daughters and that means lunch with all three, including tip, would top $80. This, you now realize, is not just a doll's tea party.

Next, we stopped by the theatre in the lower level. Here, too, advance reservations are required. I wasn't disappointed to hear that we wouldn't be able to get tickets when I saw the price – an astonishing $28 per person. Take your three daughters and you've just said goodbye to a crisp Ben Franklin note, plus a few George Washingtons. A history lesson, indeed.

Despite prices that were certainly out of reach for the vast majority of parents in our nation, the aura and atmosphere in the store and even outside of it left me even more appalled. While we stumbled from one display to the next, I noticed random dads and grandpas scattered around the place, seated in the kind of plush, upholstered chairs you typically find in luxury women's clothing stores. They rolled their eyes, wondering exactly how much this "experience" was going to cost them. Mobs of girls waited with their dolls at the doll beauty parlor, where professional stylists coiffed a smirking platoon of "Samantha" dolls – for a fee, of course. Girls clutched their distinctive American Girl Place shopping bags, eyeing one another's hauls.

Throughout the Windy City, these girls carry the bags as a badge of honor. In front of the store, the girls wear toothsome grins and wave their purchases while their mothers take photographs for posterity. What are they commemorating? I would like to know. Their daughter's first foray into conspicuous consumerism?

After 30 minutes, I'd had enough. I watched as girls wandered between artfully arranged tableaux, repeating the mantra, "Can Santa bring this for Christmas?" I gathered up my daughters and led them back to the store entrance.

"Look, girls," I beckoned, pointing across the street to the small city square. "Horse-drawn carriages. Want to take a ride?"

We walked over to the carriages, and I asked the driver how much for a ride.

"$35 for half an hour," came the reply. I did the math -- $8.75 per person.

We climbed in. For a delightful 30 minutes, we rode in the rickety carriage, listening to the sights and sounds of the city as well as the clip-clop of the horse's hooves. Down to Lake Michigan, along the shoreline, and then back to the square, where a street performer played jazz on his saxophone. The driver took our photo in the carriage, and we all piled out, laughing and relaxed.

Back home, we'll continue to enjoy our American Girl dolls. But on our next trip to the Windy City, we'll give American Girl Place a wide, wide berth.

MY BEST DAY

Rebecca Rivard

It was 1981, the Pope got shot twice, the catfights on *Dallas* were rocking our evenings, Blondie insisted "the Tide is High," and that Native American was still crying about the litter someone had dropped on the road; I was in the ninth grade. I was engulfed in the adolescent quicksand of friends with shifting loyalties, the awakening fascination/horror with my hormonal physical changes, and the fallout from my parents' divorce years earlier.

In an attempt to find my way out of the security of my books and into the social quagmire of junior high society, I committed to joining a team. Which team was not of concern for me, my ultimate goal was simply engagement with others, a way to break out of the certainty that I was being irrevocably stereotyped into nerdville. No more would I be rushing home to catch *General Hospital* to see if Luke and Laura would marry after he raped her. What was up with that? I still can't hear Herb Albert's "Rise" without crying out "no Luke, no!" Good T.V. fare to grow up on. It really was time for me to engage.

The first thing I did was get a Farrah Fawcett haircut. My hair had formerly hung down my back, just brushing the tops of my Jordache jeans; now it was feathered back in swoops all around my face. I was making progress. The only team to be planning tryouts at that "do-over" moment was the girls' basketball team. I signed up for tryouts, blissfully ignoring the fact that I had less than zero athletic ability. The closest I had come to playing the sport was watching the neighborhood high school boys shoot hoops, or the rare game of "P-I-G" where a day to celebrate was when I got the "P." I handed my physical form to perhaps the largest man I have ever seen, Mr. Thummel, the girls' basketball coach. He literally had two belts fastened together which barely met in the front; he had to be pushing four hundred pounds easily. This was the man who would train me into athleticism?

He pointed a grubby round fist toward the rest of the girls who were already running wind sprints, and I made my way toward the new group to which I hoped to belong. I gave those practices my all. I came to every practice and practiced at home. I watched the popular girls and mimicked their stretching and calf-building exercises. I had been praying since approximately the 5th grade, when my best friend got her period, that I would at least get boobs. No luck. I was still an ironing board in a little girl's body. To me, the other girls looked like Olympic Barbie and I was the little sister Skippper; a wannabe. I ran like a lunatic with spastic jerks and barren lay-ups. I tried harder to learn the grace of basketball than I have in maybe any other aspect of my life.

Finally the day came to get our uniforms. We all ran to a musty closet on the second floor of the school. In a tangled pile of possibility lay the uniforms. Yes, we re-used uniforms at our school; when you were done for the year, you simply washed your shorts and shirt and threw them back into the pile for the next year's team. I clutched the # 7 uniform to my chest, so excited to be holding the proof that I was part of a team.

The coach approached me there, while the rest of the girls were scrambling through the pile, looking for their favorite number to emblazon on their chests. He reached out his pudgy hand, squinted at me and said, "You can't have a uniform, I have to cut one person from the team." I stared at him, hope and self esteem dying in my eyes. Whaaaat??? He was exasperated that I didn't immediately comply to his crushing request. He sighed and patted down his comb-over, "We have one too many players here; you will have to give your uniform to Suzie." My mind screamed, "Suzie? The burnout? She didn't even make it to half the practices!!!" Suzie quickly grabbed the uniform out of my numb arms. Maybe I would have a heart attack right here.

I stumbled past the lockers, Farrah Fawcett locks wafting in the breeze, and collapsed in the locker room in a gale of body wracking sobs. As the other ninth grade girls filed into the locker room to change and go home, they walked by me as if I was one of those damaged animals dying on the side of the road. If they came too close, they might do more damage—or I might attack. Determined not to add shame to my many junior high labels, I pulled myself together and called my mom to come pick me up from practice. I told her nothing. It was too great and inexplicable a grief to express. The next morning I packed up my basketball practice clothes in my duffel bag and carried them out the door for the bus to school.

As I twisted the lock to my ancient locker, I wondered where I would go after school while my former teammates geared up for their first big game. The answer came as if in a prophecy. While reaching down to tie my high-top Reeboks, a flyer drifted onto the floor. "Cheerleading tryouts; practices start tonight," it proclaimed. Okay, I said, what's the worst that could happen? I get cut? Been there; and so I went. Because I had nothing to lose, I was loose and confident. I made that team even though not once did I demonstrate anything remotely resembling a cartwheel. I mentally shook my pom-poms in Suzie's carcinogenic face and shouted deep from my diaphragm so that Mr. Thummel would know I had not been defeated.

I easily consider the morning the cheerleading flyer drifted into my life one of the top five best days of my life. Not because I became a cheerleader; I dropped that "sport" at the end of ninth grade. It was my best because it clearly and profoundly illustrated that there is always a door open somewhere, that you should not let someone else determine your path, and that you should be open to and unafraid of new possibilities. Some people never even open the book to that life lesson. Although in ninth grade I wasn't allowed to join the basketball team or watch the salacious *Three's Company*, I was allowed to join a team. And let's not forget the life lesson my ninth grade self realized: a Farrah Fawcett haircut looks damn good on a cheerleader.

THE RETURN ADDRESS SAID "SPIDER-MAN"

Rebecca Rivard

I hesitantly reached into our rusty mailbox. It always had a fugitive insect concealed in its depths, waiting to pounce on my outstretched hand exactly when I reached for the missives. It was an achingly hot day, and the metal hook burned my fingers as I yanked open the little door that separated me from those messages from elsewhere. My mother's birthday was in two days, and I had been sweating the on-time delivery of the necklace I had ordered; her name, "Linda," gloriously spelled out in rhinestones. I had stuffed all of my change into an envelope with the order form and had even remembered to save enough money to buy one fifteen cent stamp; man those prices were outrageous. I even bravely ignored the aggravating assurances of my older sister that "only an idiot sends cash in the mail" accompanied by the equally subversive "it probably got stolen, moron." I had been looking for that necklace all week, waiting to stuff it in her know-it-all face.

No necklace. Okay, I still had one more day.

I half-heartedly shuffled through the other letters; maybe my new teacher's name for third grade would be in there. That would certainly spike the excitement of the day, and I could start the flurry of phone calls to my friends about their assignments; each phone call pregnant with the duplicitous possibilities of heartbreak or celebration. As I flipped through the stack, one tan crinkled envelope made me freeze right in the middle of the street.

The return address said Spider-Man.

I furtively looked around my neighborhood. Johnny Evans was ape-ishly riding his banana seat, tiger-striped bike that no one would sit on, as it was rumored that he frequently just "peed his pants" when he was too busy to bother coming in, but otherwise I was safe. He was too big of a dope and a show-off to bother noticing the top secret information I possessed.

My heart was so full. I couldn't believe it. The handwriting was unmistakable. In the center of the envelope my name marched across in my father's unmistakable engineer's scrawl, and in the return address it said "Spider-Man". I totally knew with the unimpeachable certainty of an eight year old that the US government would not allow a letter to be delivered with a false return address on it. It was true; my dad was Spider-Man. There was even a sticker of Spider-Man on the envelope.

My father had told us earlier that week that he "had to go," plunging us into a trinity of fear, confusion, and grief. He had been traveling frequently for the past year for work; we never knew when he would come or go. He choked out in a strained voice that this was not for work. He said he would contact us, but there were important reasons he had to leave. He sobbed while he packed up his button-up shirts and work pants, packing up every bit of him that proved I had a dad living there. My mom had slumped onto the strawberry printed tablecloth staring empty eyed but wet faced into the hopelessness of her future. Nobody was telling my sisters or me anything. I searched all week for a reason while people flowed through our house like voyeuristic mourners. I overheard snippets of conversations where people badgered my mom. "What will you do—a handicapped woman with no job or college degree? How will you feed these girls?" Or the sure to make my mom sob query—"Where did he meet this woman?" It was completely mystifying.

Now the mystery was SOLVED. This letter was the proof. He had to be busy saving people and that is why he couldn't live with us anymore. I wondered if he slept in a web bed and if he could make me one. More fervently, I wished he would just take me with him. I could be more helpful than he thought. I had read every Marvel series of Superheroes comic books, even the boring ones. I knew exactly what to do when faced with a supervillain, I even knew some of their lesser known weaknesses. This was going to be great. I couldn't be selfish and want him to stay because the whole world needed him. I secretly, shamefully wished for a moment that he would NOT be Spiderman, that he would just be Dad. I needed a dad.

But oh gosh, why was I just standing there? I had to tell my mom and definitely NOT tell Johnny Evans. Or maybe I should just rub it in his face. After all, his dad just worked at the tool and die. I wonder what his mom would say when she found out that my dad was a superhero—she would be so bummed that she told Johnny and his asthmatic brother Denny that they couldn't play with us since our dad moved out. Oh, this was going to make everything better. I couldn't wait to show my mom, to ease her fears. Spider-Man always came back to Mary Jane. That mystery woman must just be his boss; his traveling was clearly related to top secret missions. What a relief.

I flew through the door almost screaming with the news. "Mom, oh mom, everything is going to be okay," I exulted, "I got a letter, a real letter. I know you will have trouble believing this, but it is true!" I took a deep breath, filled with pride that I was the significant person who would bring her the saving news. Giving me a weak smile I had rarely seen that week, she mumbled, "What is going on, honey?" With shining eyes and a rush of breath, I whispered with the gravity due this situation, "Mom, the reason Dad left is because he is Spider-Man. And I have the proof right here."

As I handed her our ticket to Superfamily domestic bliss, I did not get the parade down Main Street I was expecting. My mom's face caved in as she looked at the envelope and its subsequent subversively created false identity. A small "oh" slipped from her lips. That small letter communicated a chasm between the past and the future. I watched her soul retract in her eyes as she read the lie written by a weak man who didn't want to lose his girls' love. The letter wafted to the floor, and she stumbled down the hallway and crumpled into her bed.

She did not get out again for one straight week—even when the "Linda" necklace came.

IT'S IN HIS FACE: A PORTRAIT OF SAINT MICHAEL

Isabel Vukich

When I arrive in Heaven, I expect to find a special section reserved for the saints...those whose lives were remarkable, whose acts of kindness were extraordinary, and whose hearts were made of gold. When I find this section, I believe there will be a spot reserved for my husband. Why, you ask? Is he a great humanitarian? Does he heal the sick, feed the poor, take care of orphans and widows, lead sinners to salvation? While Michael is willing and able in regards to each of these holy acts, the singular reason he deserves a seat in the saint section, closest to God, is he has faithfully and dutifully put up with.... me.

There have been tests along the way. With each of these tests I have watched my husband closely, for his face tells of the great inner struggle to maintain composure as he desperately tries to understand how and why I can make ordinary events way too eventful. The time I hit his car with my car in our driveway, for instance. Most men would not be happy about this—they'd show anger—perhaps yell. But Michael could not. His face remained still as his eyebrows danced a nervous jitter and straightened out quickly. You see, that night I was having the youth group over, youth pastors included, and they all stampeded into our home just minutes after my driveway demolition derby event.

There was the night he dragged himself home from an exhausting business trip, fraught with hassles, only to discover I accidentally flushed the stove knobs down the toilet. Since we had a family of six in the house who needed to eat and... well, pee, those knobs would have to be retrieved soon—like that very night. As Michael took off his suit, he began to ask how I could flush stove knobs down the toilet, but he stopped for he knew the answer would never suffice. So, his face took on a quiet, but confused look as he rolled up his sleeves and got busy. It's a bit funny to see a toilet removed from its place of honor.

On to the kitchen remote. Every man becomes a bit cranky when this essential gadget goes missing. For days the man scoured the usual hiding places, interrogated the children and the dog, prayed for revelation. Imagine my dismay when driving home from work one evening; I grabbed my cell phone out of my purse and realized the reason the key pad was refusing to cooperate as I dialed out was I was making a phone call with the kitchen remote. Oh God! The good news that the remote had been found was overshadowed by the realization that now I had some explaining to do regarding my cell phone. It was then I began to imagine what Michael's face might look like this time.

Dare I mention the time I was sent to the fast food restaurant, placed an order, paid, and arrived back home only to find I had no food as I had chosen to drive right past the pick-up window? It was at that point that Michael broke out in a big smile as he realized that my talent for making myself look foolish was not exclusive to our home, but was being taken out into the community. The smile did not last long before the "stare straight ahead and don't blink" look came back.

I am a bit timid when it comes to flying, so I began a tradition of meeting my husband at the Union Station in Chicago when we made our yearly trip to his company's gala in the windy city. One year the train broke down in Niles. After a few hours delay, I was relieved when we finally pulled into the station in Chicago. What I saw on Michael's face was not relief—it was pain. His tush was sore from the long hours waiting on the hard benches. Not a fair exchange for missing the evening's social mixer. The next year Michael finally put his foot down. This train trip did not fare well because somewhere around Kalamazoo we sent a 1 1/2 ton county dump truck, along with its full load of road salt, spiraling high above us after we rammed into it at an intersection. I remember watching the truck, thinking it must have been a toy the way it somersaulted into the air. I remember hearing the salt rain down on the roof. I remember seeing the mangled cow catcher at the front of the engine as we disembarked. What I remember most of all is Michael's face when I met him at the station. Eyes pressed forward, he was in total control of all facial muscles. It was at that moment I realized the next year I would be flying to Chicago with Michael.

A few years ago we took a little romantic trip to Florida. Who would think a casual lunch at an oceanside grill could lead to terror from the bushes? When out sauntered a cute little kitty, it never occurred to me not to feed it. How was I to know it was feral member of the cat crew the Marriott employed to keep the rat population under control? Was I expected to know Collier County had a rabies epidemic? Wasn't it the responsibility of the doctor at the Marco Island clinic to know and follow the protocol for wild animal bites? How might I describe Michael's face when he learned we would return to Michigan only to endure rounds of rabies shots and rabies-induced symptoms? All three of my children were sure I might die. Over the few weeks it took for the drama to die down to a *purr,* there were times when I saw Michael's face staring at mine in a way that suggested he might not mind discovering a bit of frothy foam gathering around the corners of my lips.

It took a trip to a foreign land for Michael's greatest experience with "this could only happen to Isabel" weirdness. After a day of not feeling so well—partly because I packed my heart and breathing medicine in my luggage that was lost—Michael and I sought help in a small resort clinic 100 miles from Cancun. As my symptoms escalated, the doctor made it clear he was treating me for a heart attack so Michael was forced to face my possible death. Even though this would bring him freedom from me, it apparently did not set well with my man, so he passed out—twice. Feeling foolish, and needing to arrange two ambulance rides into the Yucatan jungle to seek appropriate medical attention, Michael knew he had to put his game face back on. This time his face was not forced into a look by Michael's strong will; his face was reshaped by a puffy swollen mass caused by a fractured eye bone; the result of hitting the floor as I was "dying." Everyone who saw Michael could read his face...black, blue, purple and yellow. Before long I was admitted to Intensive Care, and Michael began a quest for solutions to the many problems my stay in a foreign hospital presented. As days passed and he wandered here and there along the streets of Cancun wearing his red bathing suit, the locals became wary of his face. Compared to the average Mayan, my husband is a big man. A big man with a black eye who hasn't shaved or changed clothes in days can be suspicious. If they looked closely, however, they would have seen the face of worry as Michael tried his best to maintain his usual cool during a time that we now call "one for the books."

To appreciate all of these escapades you have to know Michael. He is a loving and sweet man whose game face is always on. He maintains control in all situations. His is a linear world of consistent and reliable habits. Mistakes are not embraced. That he is my life partner reveals God's sense of humor. I adore this man, so I pray when our journey through this world is over I will find Michael in that special section in heaven. I wonder what his face will look like there...will it reflect the majesty of God, will it glow with serenity and peace, free from the trials of life? Yes, I think it will...that is until he realizes I am with him once again...for eternity. I pray that won't be too hard to face.

CHAPTER 3

FICTION

GALL

John Callaghan

It's 4:00 in the morning, and I'm lying on that lumpy bed, waiting to hear the sounds. I don't want to be here when he dies. My mother should be the one. I know it's just circumstances: I'm on spring break, hoping to get away from my students for awhile. I'd decided to visit my grandfather who lives some 500 hundred miles away from where I teach and I know he's old –87—but I remember him when I was a little boy, and it doesn't somehow seem right that I should be here when he dies.

The attack last night is more than any human should have to endure. I thought gall bladder attacks were internal stabs of pain, not violent vomiting and spasms of diarrhea. And he was just staring, his expression blank, as all that stuff spilled out. At least he didn't hear the two aunties whining about him making another mess.

I'm listening more intently now. I can't hear him breathing. Should I sneak a look? I don't want to wake him. I can still see him sitting at the kitchen table just 10 hours ago, his hair slicked back, his eyes rapturous with my visit. He's excited I'm visiting. I'm feeling guilty because I haven't seen him for a few years, not since Nana's funeral, and I haven't written or called in awhile. Too busy. Too distracted with teaching, coaching, family, all the events and obligations that keep me in the present, ignoring my roots, all the underpinnings that formed me into what I have become.

His voice croaks from time to time as the words spill out, memories of our visits as little kids, rides in the truck, trips to the beach, stories about me as a little boy.

I'm teasing him. "I hear you don't drive anymore, Granpa. No more rides around the loop for hot dogs and Lake Ontario sunsets."

"Well, Teddy, I'm getting on in years and don't have the need. Besides, the girls would have a fit." Still calling his sisters "the girls." I wonder what my students would think to hear someone calling me "Teddy."

So I'm lying here, his voice resonant in my head while I strain to listen for his breathing; he's down the hall, in the nook just off the kitchen where he used to spend hours reading and smoking his cigars, waiting for dinner or waiting for bed. Now he's set up closer to the bathroom, and his sisters sleep in the front room off the living room where he and Nana slept together for over 60 years.

I poke my head out into the hallway. I hear it. The breathing is steady, regular. Is he staring straight up the way I left him, his eyes out of focus—the way he was when I finally got him into that bed? I was amazed at how thick-muscled he was, and I could feel the thump-thump of his heartbeat as I bear hugged him into bed. It was the only reason I didn't call EMS. Besides, the aunties pleaded for me not to. They had the same fear they had when they were little kids so many years ago: If you left the house and entered the hospital, you never returned, except, as Nana used to say, "In a box." And, of course, that was exactly what did happen to Nana just a few years ago.

That thick strength of his comes from years and years of hard labor, fast walking wherever he went, and cheery hellos to everyone in town.

At the kitchen table earlier, he had said, "You know, I still open the store every morning."

"You still get up at 5:00, walk over there, and open up good old Gallagher Lumber Company?"

"Yep. It gives me something to do. And I don't mind it at all." Granpa shrugs his shoulders, but I know he is proud of the many years he's contributed to the business and that he is still able to help in some small way.

"Do you miss the full time work, Granpa? Last I saw you working they had you doing phone orders all day long to keep you out of the yard, throwing cement bags and 2 x 4's around. Besides, who did a better job answering the phone and taking customer orders than you? And you know everybody in town."

But Granpa doesn't hear. He is suddenly spilling forth tears, his hands clasped as though in prayer.

"I never thought she would go first. I just knew I would die before her."

"Granpa, please, it's OK..." My words stumble.

I'm embarrassed at my embarrassment. But he hears me not. He blinks at the tears, his shoulders shuddering, his clasped hands trembling with the effort to control his emotions. And I remember sitting on his lap so many years ago, the cigar smell comforting me, him putting my hands together, jamming my fingers together except for the forefingers. Those he places tip to tip, pointing them up: "Here's the church, there's the steeple, open the door, and there's all the people..."

And now his fingers spasm together, the painful memories twisting them. The church door won't open.

"I can't believe she's gone. I keep waiting to hear her voice in the kitchen, calling me to supper. Sometimes I think I see her in the corner of my eye. I'm always turning my head to see her, and she's never there. I even catch myself talking to her some times. It's over five years now, but it's like she died yesterday. The pain won't go away. I wish God would take me—get it over with."

And I sit there nodding, saying, "Yes, Granpa. Yes."

His grief shocks me. I've always known him to be such an exuberant man, full of energy and confidence. I see him in my head 20 years ago in the lumber yard, tossing boxes of nails, packages of roofing, bags of cement onto the trucks to help the delivery men, to get them moving to the customers as soon as possible. He had gotten me a summer job there as a loader and unloader—trucks, boxcars, forklifts—and Nana made me promise to keep him out of the yard. I couldn't keep my promise: he was too energetic. But I never told on him.

Now he's apologizing. "Sorry. It just came over me. She loved it when you kids visited. She'd get things ready, starting two, three weeks before you'd arrive. And we'd talk about all the things you kids would do and say, the adventures you went on, the way you'd fight over who'd sit next to the window in the truck. She never liked me driving you kids around in that old thing, you know."

"Those rides were the highlight of the day!" I plaster a smile on my face. His mouth smiles back, but his eyes don't.

An hour later we are eating an enormous meal. The aunties, Ellie and May, a few years younger than their brother, a few less wrinkles, have prepared the feast. Ellie is a spinster lady, May a widow. Granpa eats everything while Ellie tells me everything he is eating is stuff the doctor has told her is bad for his gall bladder condition: pork roast, mashed potatoes and gravy, buttery rolls, thick cream in the coffee, chocolate ice cream for dessert. Ellie says, "But he wants to celebrate your visit. He's really excited you're here. So what can we do?" They give him seconds and thirds.

An hour after dinner he explodes with the gall bladder attack. Everything comes pouring out of him from wherever anything can spew forth. The aunties whine and moan. They scold him for soiling himself and the chair he is sitting in, berating him as though he were a child. The words "dirt" and "filth" are contemptuous, petulant. He hears none of it. He only moans with the onset of the next spasm. I somehow get him cleaned up and in bed. The aunties do nothing except start the washer to clean the stuff he has befouled. "He's done this before but not this bad," May says and Ellie's head is nodding agreement. "We call his nephew, Billy. He comes over to clean it up. "

The smell overwhelms me at first, choking and gagging me, and I wish I were somewhere else. But I see him lying there, staring straight up, seeing nothing, hearing nothing. At first I think stroke. Maybe I should call for an ambulance even though I promised the aunties not to. But then I'm thinking, He wants to die, he wants to be with Nana, he has no purpose here, but don't die, Granpa, don't die. Something of me will die too like it did when Nana went, and we waked her right there in the living room. I kept expecting her to get up and sit in the chair next to the bay window and stare out that window and dream her fantasies and watch the people and cars go by while she waited for her man to come home from work, now this lonely, empty vessel of grief, who talks to her because he is so used to her presence and can't get used to her departure.

"We got to go to bed," Ellie says. "Been a long day. See you in the morning. He's real glad you're here. 'Night." They twitter and mumble and, once assured that everything is clean and that I will do something about the smell, hobble off to bed—Nana and Granpa's bed once. How must he feel about that and about this old bed they once used for guests or for our visits? So that he can get to the bathroom and not make a mess? Does he feel like a guest? Does he feel welcome? I get the Murphy's Oil Soap and the Lysol out. I scrub and spray, scrub and spray, and the stench begins to ease up. I put the washer through another cycle and then stuff everything in the dryer, always listening to the breathing, waiting for the sound. I check on him again: his breathing is regular, and he has closed his eyes, finally. So I tiptoe down the hallway, enter the guest room and lie down on the bed fully clothed, waiting, waiting.

It's probably after five now. I can see the early spring foliage out the window. Exhaustion seeps into my arms and legs, my eyes aching, my stomach clenched like an angry fist. I'm sore from the lifting and scrubbing and cleaning. I'm ready to concede to death, to let him go to Nana. If I hear the telltale sounds, the death rattle, I will go to him, hold on to those hands and tell him it's OK to let go. He's had a full life.

I begin to hear movements, quiet, careful ones, perhaps a turning over in bed, an adjustment of the sheets. I hear no distress. But what is that smell penetrating the spicy, evergreen perfume from Murphy's Oil Soap and the Lysol spray? It's familiar, somehow comforting. Something releases in my chest and bubbles up. My shoulders are heaving up and down, and I'm giggling like a little kid on his first speedboat ride. I'm striding down the hallway, coughing down my giggles, tears streaming down my cheeks.

He's sitting in the easy chair by the window, tapping the brown tube at the ashtray, in his underwear, a towel draped around his shoulders. He looks up at me, the smoke from the cigar billowing out of his mouth and nose, just like Granpa of old, except for the way he's dressed. He's smiling and his voice booms out at me, "Good morning, Teddy. Have a good night's sleep?"

LONG LIVE THE QUEEN

Linda DeCumen

Once upon a time in a far off land, well not really so far, lived a sweet and kind middle-aged Queen. The sweet and kind middle-aged Queen lived in a castle with her arrogant, middle-aged, fit-for-life King and their two beautiful, fair-haired, perfectly shaped daughters. Every day the obnoxious, in-shape King and health conscious daughters lectured the Queen about looking good and getting in shape. Each morning the dear middle-aged Queen went to the gym to work out and tried her hardest to get in shape. It seemed as though the battle was endless.

One day the lovely, middle-aged Queen hurried her breakfast down her throat and left the palace to become a fit and healthy Queen. Upon entering the gym, the good Queen tugged at her bathing suit until she finally pulled it over her wealth of curves. She stretched a cap over her lovely brown curls and raced out to the pool.

The adoring Queen set her spectacles on her towel and jumped bottom first into the shivering cold water. To her shock and dismay, the shy Queen felt something hard and blunt swimming furiously beneath her. Someone had attacked the poor Lady. She swam away from her assailant as quickly as she could. Fearing her intruder was still after her, the poor Queen ran trembling to the locker room, grabbed her clothes, threw her coat over her shoulder and sprinted to her waiting carriage.

All the way home, the feeling of violation exploded in her mind. She knew the pleasing-to-the-eye King would question her day's exercise and diet. What would she tell him? He surely wouldn't believe anyone would want to attack her, so she held her head in shame as she once again failed in her strive to lose weight.

The kind-hearted, forlorn Queen laid her head on a soft pillow and cried herself to sleep. The Queen awoke startled. Sitting beside her was a woman who mirrored the image of Oprah Winfrey! She appeared more beautiful than Oprah, and she kept smiling at the Queen. "Who are you?" asked the inquisitive Queen.

"I am your Fairy Food-mother, Oprah, but you can call me Fairy O."

"Oh Fairy O, I am in such distress. You see, I have two beautiful daughters and a handsome husband who are in perfect shape, and, well, the problem is that I cannot keep up my beauty any longer. I struggle and work so hard to keep in shape, but I always fail. Moreover, the King and my daughters ridicule my weakness and laugh at my clumsy exercising and body fat. What am I to do, Fairy O?" cried the distressed Queen.

"Do not give it another thought," replied Fairy O. "I will send my trainer, Bob, to help you. You will find happiness once again, my dear Queen."

"Oh Fairy O, you are 'The great and powerful O,' and I will. . ." but before the pleasant Queen could speak another word, Fairy O was gone, and the doorbell was ringing. The good, middle-aged Queen shook her head, wiped the sleep from her eyes and ran to the door. Standing in front of her was the exercise guru, Bob.

The startled queen was taken aback, and tears welled up in her eyes. "Fairy O is real, and she has saved my life," wailed the precious Queen. Exercise guru, Bob, made her drop and give him 10. The humble, middle-aged Queen did exactly that. She actually could do that! She looked in the mirror and chanted, "Mirror, Mirror on the wall, who's the fairest Queen of all?"

"Why you," replied the mirror.

The Queen was slim and beautiful as she once was. "What happened to me?" the queen shouted with glee. The Queen decided not to question this wonderful fate and thanked Bob; then, she began making dinner.

The egotistical King came home and sat in the dining room waiting for his dinner. The irreverent daughters also sat at the table waiting for the Queen to serve them. As the newly attractive Queen set the fresh greens on the table, her family gave little reference to her entry. As they each looked up, one at a time, they sat with their mouths open without breathing a word.

Finally, the arrogant King stood up and demanded to know what had happened to the Queen; how had she lost weight so quickly and turned back time with her youthful looks? The Queen told her family of her day at the pool, her sleep, Fairy O and trainer Bob. They all laughed so hard; they almost fell off their chairs.

The beautiful middle-aged Queen stood up at the dining room table and made an announcement. She told the overconfident King and her conceited daughters that she found a new life, and she would be leaving the kingdom. The excited middle-aged Queen smiled as her new love entered the room. She explained to the King and her daughters that she needed a change. She intended to travel to other parts of the country and help other middle-aged women. The Queen would convey that life goes on when you get to that *time in your life* when your body becomes defiant. "It is now my time to make others happy, others who will appreciate me," she declared.

The Queen and her new love, trainer Bob, went around the world offering advice and hope to middle-aged women. After each rally, the women always chanted, "Long Live the Queen." The fit Queen and Bob lived happily ever after.

GRANDPA'S SHOES

Kim Grusecki

I have passed on this story numerous times over the years. Subsequently, it has become the stuff of urban legends, with the tree considered a local attraction. Visitors today can see the tree located just minutes from my home. It is now filled with numerous gifts from the various visitors in loving tribute or from those just looking for a blessing from above.

When I was in seventh grade, Grandpa came to live with us. Just before he came, there was a flurry of activity. Mom was rushing about cleaning out the junk room. There were boxes everywhere, and I could smell fresh paint when I came down the hallway.

"Whatcha doin?" I asked when I peeked my head into the room.

"Grandpa's coming today!" smiled Mom. "I have to put the finishing touches on the room. Hurry and grab your sweatshirt. The bus is almost here."

I dashed out the front door as the bus came bounding down the dirt road. I could hear the sound of crunching stones and hydraulic brakes squeaking. The door made a rusty sound as it opened and I shouted, "See ya!" to basically no one as the doors closed behind me.

While I was at school, Grandpa arrived with all of his belongings and moved into the now ex-junk room. His health had gone downhill since Grandma passed on, and after a big family meeting it was decided he would come to our house and stay.

When I got home from school, Grandpa was seated on his bed with his cane in hand. He had hung up a few shirts in his closet and set out some old pictures. The one of Grandma as a young bride was by his bedside. The window was half-open and an ever-so-slight breeze was blowing in. All of his shoes were lined up in the closet. At the end of the row of perfectly aligned shoes was a box that contained his "special shoes." For what purpose, he never explained.

As far as I know no one ever really said what tribe Grandpa was from, but all I know is that he had an odd way of speaking. He was very kind, but I always thought he wasn't very bright. You could never carry on a conversation with him. Whenever he spoke, he said some weird off-the-wall kind of stuff that left people scratching their heads, feeling sorry for him and just kind of evaporating from the room.

"Hey, Grandpa! How's it going? It's so nice to have you here." Grandpa smiled a genuine smile. "Do you think you'll be happy here?" I asked, tempting fate and beginning a conversation.

"Happiness is a state of mind," replied Grandpa. I paused to roll that remark around in my brain. I knew he would say something dumb like that. "Can't argue with that," I replied brightly. "Well, I gotta go," I said taking off to play outside. See, I told you he wasn't the brightest light bulb in the pack.

Grandpa's presence wasn't very disruptive and life seemed to fall into a regular routine. The school year seemed to blow by uneventfully and quickly while Grandpa's health continued on a steady decline. He wasn't really sick. He just seemed to be more sad, forgetting things and becoming much less energetic.

One Saturday Mom and Dad really needed to go out shopping. With Christmas right around the corner, they had a million errands to run. Mom sat me down and asked me if I would keep an eye on Grandpa. "Of course, I will!" I said enthusiastically, hoping to make some Christmas brownie points.

"You have the emergency phone numbers, right?"

"Yes, mother," I said condescendingly.

"Don't be smart," she said. "You know Grandpa hasn't been feeling well," Mom added, almost whispering.

"O.K." I said. "This is important. I get it."

"Dad and I will try not to be long," said Mom.

"Go on. It will be fine," I said a little nervously. Mom was kind of creeping me out.

So, Mom and Dad left. I went to goof around quietly in my room. Grandpa slept until about 11:00. When he got up, he slowly came down the hallway to get his morning cup of coffee and drink it with his usual two pieces of buttered toast.

"Here's the paper, Grandpa." I said joining him in the kitchen and handing it to him gently. He smiled at me and started to look it over. "Mom and Dad are out Christmas shopping." Grandpa nodded. "For Christmas, I am asking for a Penney's gift certificate and a video game to go with my Nintendo game system!" I blurted out.

"Be careful what you ask for, you might just get it," said Grandpa.

Mom had started referring to Grandpa as having "good days" and "bad days". This must be what she meant by one of his "bad days." I decided to make the best of it, though, in hopes that I would be rewarded well on Christmas Day.

"I am doing pretty good in school," I said trying to start up a conversation again. "So far this marking period, I have mostly A's and B's." Grandpa looked up from his paper briefly and replied, "Brains are better than brawn."

O.K. Wow! This is going to be, like, a lot tougher than I thought. Guess I'll shift the conversation off me. Hmmmm. "So, do you still like living here, Grandpa?"

"Be it ever so humble, there's no place like home."

Boy, I really don't think Grandpa is all there. "I'm gonna go back and mess around in my room now," I said as I walked away leaving Grandpa at the kitchen table to work the crossword puzzle in peace.

The winter passed by uneventfully, but when spring arrived, Grandpa was down to about 90 pounds. Sadness and weakness seemed to engulf him. Every morning like clockwork though, he got up, inched his way slowly down the hallway in his pajamas and robe to have his morning coffee and toast. The rest of the day, he spent either taking a walk to the woods near our home or watching television in his bedroom. Today was different though.

Today, Grandpa got up like usual around 11:00 and inched his way down the hallway. Instead of his pajamas, he was completely dressed already! He had on one of his shirts from his closet and a pair of dress pants. Instead of slippers, he had on a pair of old moccasins with elaborate beading on the top and bottom.

I ran to Grandpa's room and looked in the closet. The box at the end of the neat row of shoes was torn open and tissue paper was strewn about the floor! I raced back to the kitchen and asked Grandpa what was going on? Grandpa replied, "A man's got to do what a man's got to do." Though that dumb answer held no meaning for me, apparently it meant something to Mom and Dad. A cold blew over the kitchen unlike anything that I had ever felt before. Mom and Dad stiffened but didn't say a word.

On that day, Grandpa slowly walked to the woods near our house. There was a tree there that had a spirit that Grandpa liked to visit. He called it "The World Tree." It is believed in some Native American cultures, that a World Tree was a tree whose limbs were connected to the Heavens and whose roots were connected to the Underworld. It was custom to throw important items up into the tree in order to receive heavenly blessings. As Grandpa stood before the tree, he removed his shoes and knelt to pray. When he finished his final communion with the tree, he gathered up his special shoes and threw them up into its loving arms.

That was the day that Grandpa offered up his soles and soul to The World Tree.

Weeks later as Mom, Dad, and I cleaned out Grandpa's room, there was again a flurry of activity in there. Since it was the weekend, I was commissioned to help. It was my job to clean out the closet. I took Grandpa's few shirts off the hangers and folded them neatly. I gathered up his shoes and put them into a bag for donation. I grabbed the box that held his sacred burial shoes. I was about to pitch it into the trash when I noticed some words scrawled on the inside cover. The words read,

"Don't judge any man until you have walked a mile in his moccasins."

It was then that it dawned on me that my Grandpa wasn't senile. He was really a great man of wisdom and truth. I was the one who didn't get it. His words were wise, but his actions spoke even louder than his words. Suddenly, the revelations kept coming! When he threw his shoes up into the tree, Grandpa wasn't giving up or getting ready to die. He was leaving a legacy. It was "through" his shoes that he was passing on his heritage and culture to the world and me!

"Duh!" I said aloud. It was then that I realized that I could be so dumb sometimes!

A Place for Lost Soles

Kim Grusecki

Bikers hiking into the woods near Dixborough Road in South Lyon late yesterday uncovered an unusual sight. Ryan and Ethan Grusecki of Washington, Michigan, were dumbfounded when they came upon the local phenomena known as "The World Tree."

According to local residents, The World Tree came into existence over twenty years ago when an aged Native American man decided that the tree was sacred. He prepared for death by throwing his last pair of moccasins up into the tree. According to legend, the Native American gentleman went to the tree, prayed his final prayer, threw his shoes into its limbs and went home to die. He was never seen again.

Out of respect for the Native American's symbolic gesture, area residents went to the tree and threw up their favorite shoes and/or other special trinkets. As the legend was passed down, people continued to visit the tree and symbolically adorn it with their old shoes and gifts. Over the years, the tree accumulated more shoes than leaves and became a local attraction.

Ryan and Ethan Grusecki said that the tree was quite a sight to behold. It stopped them right in their tracks because they had never seen anything like it. Now, the two bikers may end up being the last to visit the allegedly sacred site. Mayberry Builders of Novi announced during the January South Lyon City Council meeting that plans for a residential subdivision are currently underway. The new building project is to begin in late September once the land is cleared. The World Tree is set to be axed this fall barring public outrage.

The honored place for lost soles may soon disappear, but the people of South Lyon have vowed that the legend will not be lost. Grassroots organizations to keep the legend alive are already forming, and interested residents can contact the South Lyon City Manager, Rodney L. Cook, for more information.

As for the bikers, Ryan and Ethan Grusecki were honored to have seen the tree, and they, too, offered up their sneakers in respect. "It's the least we could do," they said as they left their soles behind and continued on their journey barefoot.

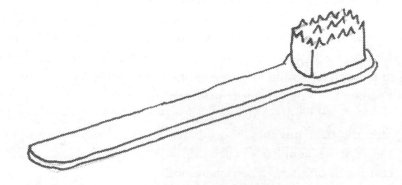